Fundamentals of Female Dynamics

Michael Knight

First Printing, 2016

ISBN-13: 978-0692655160
ISBN-10: 0692655166
True Anomaly Press

www.trueanomaly.org

Table of Contents

Preface: The Feynman Principle

"The first principle is that you must not fool yourself— and you are the easiest person to fool."
-Richard Feynman

If I had to attribute the creation of this book to one person, it would have to be the Nobel Prize winning physicist and general all-around badass Richard P. Feynman. When he was not crushing it in the field of particle physics, Feynman spent time exploring his other interests which included travel, playing drums, painting and meeting women. I first read the book *Surely You're Joking, Mr. Feynman: Adventures of a Curious Character* while attending university, and the chapter in which Feynman was taught how to pick-up women by an illiterate bartender became forever ingrained in my memory. Little did I know then, but a seed had been planted in my mind which would later sprout into a life filled with travel and adventure.

During my time at university, any remnant of a social life quickly evaporated. Keeping halfway decent grades required me to spend most weekends buried deep inside the library. Not only did the engineering environment turn out not to be very conducive to meeting women, but it also provided me with an incredibly narrow worldview. I lived for years in a bubble, where the only thing that others around me seemed to care about was scholastic achievement. I thought that there must be more to life than earning points by making marks on a sheet of paper. However, no one else around me seemed interested in finding out what else life had to offer. They all appeared content to go through each day as if they were sitting on an assembly line which emptied into the cubicle containers where they were to spend the rest of their lives.

At least this was the case until my junior year, when I was assigned a female lab partner. I could tell from the start that this girl was different from the other students. Although she excelled in the system, she did not buy into it to the same degree as everyone else. I greatly admired her independence and determination to do as she pleased. On a much deeper level, she was an embodiment of the freedom that I was unconsciously craving. However, this pursuit was to end in heartbreak and failure, as I proceeded to make every mistake in the book when it comes to attracting a woman. The greatest mistake being that I was searching for salvation in another person rather than finding it within myself.

At the end of four years, I was completely fed up with my state of affairs, and could not stand to remain on the conveyor belt any longer. Upon graduating — dissatisfied with what had become the status quo of my life and longing for a change — I packed a bag and left the United States. I have been primarily traveling and living abroad ever since.

***

One night in Poland, I met a group of five girls at a dance club. After sitting and talking with them for a while, I noticed that the drink of the cutest girl sitting across from me was empty in addition to my own. I asked her if she would like to go to the bar with me to get another drink. She said "yes," and we proceeded to go over to the bar and place our orders. I was about to pay for both of our drinks when the Feynman story re-entered my head.

In short, the Feynman story advocates never paying for a woman that you just met. A notion I thus justly refer to as the "Feynman principle." At first, this may sound incredibly counterintuitive. You are probably asking yourself the question: "Why shouldn't I pay for a girl that I like?" I thought the same, but in this instance decided to go against my social programming — which at the time felt completely wrong — and pay only for my own drink.

The girl was stunned when I did not offer to pay for her. She was so sure that I was going to buy her a drink, that she had left her wallet at our table on the other side of the dance floor. She thus had to embarrassingly walk back to her friends to fetch her purse, leaving the bartender holding her beverage.

During the remainder of the night, we hardly spoke and her friends repeatedly called me an asshole for not paying for her. However, later when we were all leaving the venue and kissing each other goodbye on the cheeks (as is the custom among acquaintances in Poland), the girl that I had embarrassed whispered to me that I owed her a real kiss. We then proceeded to make out.

By taking a chance and applying a principle that then went against my current intuition and world model, success was found. I realized that if I was wrong about the consequences behind the simple act of buying a girl a drink, then I likely still held many other false beliefs. By applying the Feynman principle, even while not yet fully understanding the deeper core principles at play, I was able to achieve dramatic results. These results served as the catalyst for my further delving into the science behind attraction. I began to devour books and other material regarding attraction and test all my prior assumptions. This fascination culminated in me traveling the world and coaching alongside some of its top dating instructors. The results of what I have learned over years of investigation are clearly laid out for you in this book.

With my newfound understanding, it is now clear to me why the Feynman principle is effective. The issue is not the actual act of buying a woman a drink, but what the act sub-communicates and one's intentions behind it. When you offer to buy a woman that you barely know a drink, it often carries with it a clear connotation. You are communicating that you are willing to provide material possessions in exchange for attention, affection and/or potential sexual favors. Even if you tell yourself that you don't actually want to sleep with the woman, you are still sending her the message: "Please take this gift and like me." While you may believe that you are offering an altruistic gift, in reality you are still in fact asking for something in return. You desire that your gift will be met by a positive response or at the very least recognition. If you believed that you yourself were of value, then you would not feel the need to provide immediate material compensation to a woman with whom you want to converse.

After receiving an unsolicited gift from a man that she does not know, some women will immediately be made uncomfortable by the feeling that they owe you something in return. Other women, who are of the type that are constantly seeking validation, will smile and thank you before leaving you to seek further validation elsewhere. Regardless of how the woman accepts your gift, you may immediately place yourself at a disadvantage by establishing an initial frame in which you are overtly trying to sell yourself.

You can just as effectively signal your interest to a woman without also offering a bribe. Do not misinterpret this lesson and believe that the point is never to buy a woman a drink. Again, the issue is not the action itself, but rather what is being sub-communicated. There are certainly situations where it is appropriate to pay for a woman, e.g. she has already bought you a drink or the drink comes from a place where you are not giving to get something in return. However, it is necessary for the woman to perceive this as the case. Often by initiating a conversation by offering to purchase a drink for a woman, the woman will automatically group you in with the other 95% of guys who do it to barter for her attention. Thus to prevent being pegged as one of these men, I have found that not buying a drink is the correct decision the vast majority of the time when initially interacting with a woman that I do not yet know.

What is most important is that you are effectively communicating the honest intent behind your actions. If you do want something in return for the drink — that is fine — but your expectations must be honestly communicated to the woman from the start. This was the surprising discovery that Feynman made when he outright asked a woman if she would sleep with him prior to buying her a drink. Likewise, if a woman asks you why you refuse to buy her a drink, tell her your honest reason for not doing so. I personally say to such women: "Don't take it personally, but I do not buy women that I just met drinks. I believe it can send the wrong message." This response is usually met by a short look of surprise, followed by a smile and the woman becoming intrigued.

The Feynman story also advocates being ungentlemanly towards women that you are interested in. Again, while Feynman was correct in observing that one can achieve successful results by employing such tactics, he does not delve deep enough and address the first principles which explain why being disrespectful can be effective. I personally do not believe that it is ever necessary to be purposely disrespectful to other people. However, I fully understand why being disrespectful seems to yield positive results with women. An understanding of the deeper fundamental principles regarding attraction reveals the truth behind the popular belief that women love assholes.

Most women that have had a half-way decent childhood are not attracted to men who are mean, self-centered, arrogant, obnoxious or indifferent towards others. Instead, it is the underlying complementary characteristics that often go with being an asshole that account for why women are attracted to them. Fortunately for humanity, these positive and attractive characteristics are not mutually exclusive to being an asshole. One can cultivate these positive attributes separately from the other negative traits.

Self-centeredness can be a characteristic of a man who is fervently pursuing what he deems as his purpose in life. Arrogance often correlates with a man who has great belief in himself. An obnoxious person typically believes that what he has to say holds value. Appearing indifferent can be a trait of a man who has abundance and is secure in his environment. Thus women are not attracted to assholes per se, but instead to confident men, who are secure with themselves, know and go for what they want and do not let the opinions of others faze them.

As previously discussed, a nice guy's actions can often be interpreted by a woman as an attempt to buy her affection. Thus inversely, being disrespectful to a woman is the clearest way of communicating that you are indifferent to her opinion of you. After all, a woman who has not read this book would likely find it hard to rationalize why a man interested in her would be insulting. An insult can sub-communicate to a woman that you are not trying to impress her or are emotionally dependent on her validation. Thus the woman will not sense that you have an agenda and will be more likely to trust what you say as being honest.

While I do not advocate actively insulting women, you should not be filtering your true thoughts and beliefs in an attempt to impress a woman or tell her what you think she wants to hear. When a woman senses that you are stuck in your head and filtering your words, she loses the sense that she can fully trust what you say and realizes that your emotions are dependent on her validation.

Conversely, when a woman senses that your emotions are not dependent on her validation, an immense pressure is removed from the interaction. Through removing one's filters and ceasing to seek approval, you will gain the trust and respect of most women. In general, women will more often be intrigued by your honesty than upset that you don't share same exact opinions as them.

A woman likes a guy who is an asshole because he communicates honest signals. She can trust that he is not putting on some type of act, and that the man she is getting to know is actually who he says he is. The actions of a so called "nice guy" are often extremely dishonest. By pretending that you are not interested in a woman, and that you are only being nice, you are effectively lying to the woman. There is incongruence between your thoughts, words and actions. This incongruence shows the woman that although you like her, you lack self-confidence, crave her validation, and want an intact ego more than you want her. To be clear, the goal is not to become an asshole, but to learn to communicate your honest intent. The types of women for whom you actually need to become an asshole to attract are the same ones that you should probably avoid.

The final lesson presented in the Feynman story is that one should simply ask for what he wants, i.e. one should make their true intentions clear. In Feynman's case, it was straight up asking a woman if she would have sex with him prior to paying for her drink. Feynman was astounded that such an action worked. Like Feynman, you too are probably wondering how being so blatant and crass can actually yield positive results. Again, we must consider what such a blatant statement sub-communicates to a woman. Such a statement undoubtedly depicts a man as showing honest intent, being unapologetic for his desires, and congruence between his thoughts, words and actions. These are all traits which women find highly attractive.

However, it is also of paramount importance to note the context in which Feynman employed this tactic. Feynman had already established attraction with these women, and asking if they would sleep with him was not so much of a request, but rather a retort to a woman implying that she could manipulate him into giving her what she wants. What most likely crossed these women's minds was: "Wow, this guy just straight-up called me out. No one ever does that... He must be of high value and thus may be actually worth getting to know." Straight up proposing such a transaction to a woman who neither has prior interest in you, nor has first tried to exploit you for a drink, will most likely just get you slapped.

The science behind attraction is an area that even a Nobel Prize winning physicist was clueless about before being schooled by an illiterate bartender. The information presented in this book will likely go against what you have previously been conditioned to believe. I recommend that you set aside preconceived notions when reading and applying the knowledge contained in the following chapters, just as I had to when I first applied the "Feynman principle" in Poland. A single chapter of a physicist's memoir profusely changed my life. I hope the contents of this book will do the same for you.

Chapter 1: Accepting a New Paradigm

"Insanity is doing the same thing over and over and expecting different results."
-Attributed (perhaps wrongly) to Albert Einstein

Hold on Dorothy, because your world is about to be turned completely upside down. The entire model upon which you base your theory of attraction is most likely fundamentally flawed. I will take the liberty of making the safe assumption that if you have decided to pick up this book, then there is a good chance that you lack success in this particular area of your life. You may be asking yourself the question: "What the heck am I doing wrong?" My personal answer to you would likely be: "Almost everything!" However, do not despair. At one time I too knew almost nothing about what women actually find attractive.

Many academics and other technically minded individuals have large egos built around being correct, and can have issues with acknowledging past mistakes. It can be incredible difficult to let go of a worldview that has been the foundation upon which you have based decisions your entire life. Without the personal life experiences to reinforce the principles in this book, the advice may seem counterintuitive and even paradoxical. However, as Richard Feynman states:

"The 'paradox' is only a conflict between reality and your feeling of what reality 'ought to be.'"

And:

"It doesn't matter how beautiful your theory is, it doesn't matter how smart you are. If it doesn't agree with experiment, it's wrong."

The discomfort that comes with relinquishing a strongly fortified belief system can be so great that it forces you to completely reject a new paradigm. Some people would rather cover their ears and run screaming from the room instead of hearing the truth. You may need to come to terms with the fact that the past could have been different if you had only taken action earlier and possessed the following information. While the past cannot be changed, you can use it as leverage to change the future. After all, the past has brought you to this current point, and from this point forward you can head in whatever direction you choose.

So clearly you desire to be better with women, but in what ways have you ever tried varying your behavior in order to better your results? My personal guess would be that you have previously done little, if anything at all. Getting wasted every Friday night with the same three friends and then stumbling up to girls and asking their names is not a recipe for success. Albeit, it is still slightly better than deciding to sit at home and do nothing at all. While dressing yourself better and hitting the gym are good starting points, your results will continue to be negligible if the fundamental axioms upon which you base your theory of attraction are completely false. Without a correct working model of what actually generates attraction in women, you will never be able to achieve consistent and repetitive results.

Many resources currently exist for the purpose of training men to become better with women. While the majority of these resources focus on describing in-depth the surface level actions that you should take, they ignore the deeper first principles from which these actions should unconsciously be derived. In contrast, this book focuses on conveying the fundamental principles behind attraction and building a solid core inner belief system. Without the right inner belief system, consistent personal growth will not be possible.

This is not to say that aspects such as eye contact, vocal tonality, and body language are not important. However, while these aspects make a difference, they do not make the difference. A person's core beliefs will always shine through their outer persona, particularly in the long run. Furthermore, poor body language and other idiosyncratic and insecure behaviors are often a reflection of one's internal personal beliefs. Thus the correcting of one's outer persona — without addressing their internal insecurities — will only ever result in temporary and fleeting successes. However, rebuilding oneself from the core out will result in the majority of these minor details taking care of themselves. Additionally, focusing on core principles will prevent you from becoming overwhelmed with trying to simultaneously address hundreds of small details all at once.

The initial few chapters of this book focus on the internal and external forces which have resulted in you arriving where you are currently at today. By first understanding the reasons why you are unsuccessful with women, we can then proceed to address the key factors at the heart of the issue instead of just trying to cover up the symptoms. The goal is to actually become an attractive man and not just learn to act like one.

You may be a man in your late teens/early twenties and enrolled at a university. If so, then the understanding and knowledge you will gain from this book is going to put you way ahead of the curve. I only wish that I had had this knowledge myself while partaking in my own studies. However, no one was there to show me the way, and if you are also currently studying a major such as computer science or engineering, then you may lack good resources as well.

Perhaps you are no longer a student, but a bit older and have been bewildered by women your entire life. In this case, hopefully this book will finally illuminate for you a subject in which you have previously been left in the dark. Most men are never taught the information contained in this book, while simultaneously remaining in environments which greatly hinder their ability to learn it. Adding on top of this, the drastic fallacies and misinformation regarding courtship promoted by the mainstream media, it is no surprise that so many men feel left out of the game.

Take a look around the environments in which you primarily spend your time and ask yourself: "Who here is super successful with women?" If the answer is almost no one, then you have just run into your first barrier to success.

The typical thermodynamics lecture or defense contractor cubicle farm is normally stocked full of individuals which likely share the same shortcomings as you. Thus day in and day out your bad habits and limited mindset are constantly being reinforced by your group of peers. There may not even be a single person in your immediate environment that can set a good example of how you can improve yourself. If this is the case, then you may be entering a tailspin that is headed towards the ground. This book is the ejector seat which can save your love life.

There are very few things that remain constant in the world. Most things are in a perpetual state of change, with the world favoring the most adaptable. Empires, Fortune 500 companies, sport franchises and one's personal health are usually either in a state of ascent or decline. Breaking a downward cycle can be incredibly difficult and require a great amount of effort and time. However, there is no better time than the present to begin paddling yourself out of a downward vortex and into an upward climb.

The longer you wait, the more inclined you may be to accept that being bad with women is just a natural part of who you are. This is not the case! You are likely just uneducated and inexperienced in regards to the topic of attraction. Many individuals choose to give up and just accept what they consider as fate. It is far easier after all to label oneself as being hopeless at something, than to work towards improvement. In this case, you will end up with not less, but exactly with what you deserve. You are insane to think that your results will change when all other variables remain the same.

But do not worry, you do not need to change your interests, join the football team, or become someone you are not. Neither do you need to disrespect and belittle women or rely on a set of routines or scripts. Instead, you just need to become the best version of yourself. While there are no absolute laws to attracting women, there are many core principles that when internalized will dramatically improve your results. Operating with an accurate understanding of the world is first required before you will be able to excel.

I do not expect everyone to immediately accept the fundamental principles recorded in this book. You should absolutely test them and perceive the results for yourself. I expect that some readers will cling to their flawed beliefs; fearing the change that comes with adopting a new paradigm. Many people subconsciously fear success, because success leads to change and change can be scary. It may take these readers many more years of failure before potentially coming to terms with reality. Some may never come to terms and continue down a path of self-delusion.

The longer you buy into a false paradigm, the harder it becomes to give it up. It can be incredibly hard to let go of something in which you have invested great amounts of energy and effort, since doing so would be admitting that the investment was a waste. This is the reason why people continue to send Nigerian prince scam artists money every month for years, instead of choosing to accept the painful realization that they have been tricked. Instead of grasping at illusions, you need to immerse yourself in cold hard reality.

We all need world models so that we can process information and make decisions. While some models are incredible useful, others are outdated, and some are just plain wrong. Even inaccurate models can on the surface still appear correct. Prior to the discovery that the Earth was not the center of the universe, star charts still allowed sailors to navigate with relative precision. However, such a model definitely had its limits. A paradigm shift clarifying that the Earth actually orbits the Sun was required before Man could successfully land on the Moon. Similarly, a paradigm shift might be required before you can land a girlfriend.

In many cases, our model for understanding something is simplified as much as our necessity for understanding it allows. For example, most people know that pushing on a gas pedal will make a car drive faster, but they have no idea about the intricate inner workings of a car. In the case of driving a car, this model is sufficient for most people since they are able to apply it effectively and in doing so get from point A to point B. However, when it comes to attraction, the mainstream societal model that the majority of men are adhering to is deeply flawed.

Many men feel that since they don't fit certain standards described by society's model, that they are undeserving of getting the attention of women. Other men continuously try to mold themselves to fit the conventional societal model, and yet never see any results. They continue down the same path, expecting that once they reach a certain level of success, that women will start finding them attractive. If you are repeatedly not getting the intended results for the actions that you are taking, perhaps it is time to consider that your world model regarding attraction is wrong.

Let's first describe the attraction paradigm by which the vast majority of people in society operate, starting with how the mainstream media depicts the stereotypical attractive man. Normally this man is rich, famous and/or good looking. While it would be delusional to think that these traits have no impact, they are not the core attributes that generate attraction in women. The primary reason these men are successful with women is that they act with confidence drawn from the fact that society gives them permission to be with attractive women. More importantly, they give themselves permission to be with these women.

In contrast, what does our society tell the nerdy engineer who has a crush on the blonde cheerleader in his math class? Is he told that he should push his comfort zone, work on improving himself and develop a deep inner self-confidence? Nope, he is instead told to just wait and that love will eventually come and find him. This is one of the most harmful messages that this person could receive. Real life is not a Lifetime movie where the girl finally comes around in the end. The message to sit and do nothing is not the advice that one should follow who is looking to change their life circumstances.

Many of those who have achieved wealth or fame have worked extremely hard to reach their current positions. Their strong determination and living a life of their choosing are traits that are much more attractive than the wealth and fame are alone. We often celebrate their successes while overlooking the long journey and failures along the way that brought them to where they are. In these cases, wealth and fame are often byproducts of achievement. Albeit, our current celebrity culture makes me think that this is becoming less and less the case. I attribute this growth in faux celebrity to a growing consumer culture focused on excessively extracting wealth from the masses whose basic needs are already met.

By promoting random reality TV stars, whose unremarkable lives can easily be emulated by anyone who is willing to spend money on expensive products and services, wealth can be effectively extracted from one's audience. Fame, status and success are thus diluted and made into an expensive yet easily purchasable product. The greatest irony is when certain products are promoted by celebrities such as athletes, whose own success would be hampered if they actually consumed the products. Drinking a sugary elixir will make you fat, not throw a ball further.

The false paradigm that looks, status and wealth alone will bring you quality women is heavily propagated by the media because it is the most effective form of advertising. It's the traditional "give me your money and I will immediately give you what you want" ploy targeted at Man's most fundamental desires. Almost all men have one thing in common, and that is a desire to be successful with women. By tapping into this desire, men are coaxed into spending their entire lives working for someone else, instead of ever working on themselves. They are told to focus entirely on earning money now with which they can purchase love later.

We are told that if we spend money on an exercise contraption, we can have rock-hard abs without having to go to the gym. We are told that if we give a financial guru our money, he will make us rich quick. We are told that if we go into debt to live an extravagant lifestyle, women will be lining up at our doors. We have all seen ads for jewelry in which an attractive woman throws herself at a man who presents her with an expensive gift; only reinforcing the false paradigm that affection can be bought. We are repeatedly told the lie that we can buy our way into being an attractive man.

While some men try to buy a woman's affection via material possession, other men choose the route of becoming self-sacrificing. These men think that they can earn a woman's affection by responding to her every beck and call. They think that by repeatedly showing their willingness to sacrifice themselves for a woman, she will eventually come to appreciate them. However, this is a one-sided commitment of which the woman has not been informed and has no reason to uphold. While some woman may take advantage of these men, most never ask for what these men do for them. These women especially resent when the men perform unrequested favors and then in return expect something for them. By mistakenly believing that they can earn a woman's affection, these men often become upset when their unsolicited sacrifices are never reciprocated. Women don't want the shirt off a man's back, but for a real man to be under that shirt.

At university, I had a friend named Ryan. Ryan had never had a girlfriend and was desperate for a woman's attention. Ryan would offer to help any girl who was having trouble with her homework assignments. He would often sacrifice completing his own work in order to help another female student finish her assignments on time. While it is one thing to help out a fellow student, it is another to continuously sacrifice your own work in the process. Some of these girls ended up failing their final exams, having not learned the material because Ryan had done the majority of their assignments for them.

It was clear to me that it was Ryan's hope that he might earn the affection of one of these girls through the act of continuously sacrificing himself for her. Ryan tried to buy affection by trading the only thing of value which he believed that he had to offer: himself. It did not surprise me that none of these women ever pursued a relationship with Ryan. By continually sacrificing your personal integrity for a woman, you are abdicating the very attributes which women desire in a man. By completely giving yourself away, you leave nothing left to be loved.

If you have also bought into the standard attraction paradigm, it will be necessary to reformat your brain and install an updated belief system. Given that neither wealth, fame nor model looks are necessary to attract women — what factors do count? Women want genuine men with confidence, passion and purpose; traits that can't be purchased but only cultivated through experience.

The following three beliefs must be ingrained in your mind before success with women can be achieved.

1. Attraction is not a choice.
2. Being able to attract women is a learnable skillset.
3. Failing does not equate to failure.

Firstly, attraction is not a choice. Think of a woman that you find attractive. While you can consciously choose to act on that attraction, you cannot choose to turn the feeling off. It is automatic and triggered by a combination of the woman's looks and personality. Likewise, a woman does not consciously choose to find you attractive. Fortunately for men, most women find a man's physical looks less important than his personality. Just as a man is automatically drawn to a woman who has a nice figure, women are drawn to men who show specific behavioral traits. While men often instantaneously find a woman attractive because of her appearance, women must collect further circumstantial evidence to judge a man's attractiveness. When you cultivate the attractive personality traits described in this book, the percentage of women who find you attractive will greatly increase.

Secondly, becoming better with woman is a learnable skillset. Most men do not know that they can learn to become better with women. However, after giving it some thought, it should become obvious. If you can go to the gym and better your physical appearance, why would it not be possible to build a more attractive personality? Learning to attract women is a social skill, and as with any other type of skill, it can be improved through proper theory and training. While certain individuals will naturally be more inclined to picking up the skill than others, anyone who puts in the effort can increase their competency.

While this book hopefully contains many great epiphanies which will drastically increase your understanding of attraction, it is still not a magic pill. You will still need to practice applying the principles in this book with actual women to see improvement. Experience will always trump pure theory. There is also a difference between knowing something and truly internalizing it. You can perfectly memorize the theory presented in this book, but until you put it into action, your results will not change. Michael Jordan could teach you the theory behind a perfect jump shot, but you still must train your muscles how to properly respond for your shots to improve. The more you interact with women, and the more references experiences you gain, the greater your intuition and social intelligence will grow.

Lastly, one has to have the mentality that failing does not equate to failure. Your journey will not be a road paved solely with success. It is supposed to be difficult at times. As with gaining anything in life that is worth having, you will need to put in the work. As long as you are honestly working to better yourself, you should never feel disappointed. Your mantra should be: "I either succeed or I learn." From every failure there is embedded a lesson which can be applied to bring you future success. In the end, the journey is often sweeter than the final destination, although it may not seem so at certain instances of time.

The process of self-improvement is incredibly rewarding and you will even learn to embrace the struggle. Resistance and failure are preludes to growth. You only gain muscle when you push yourself a bit further than you have previously before. Every barrier you clear puts you closer to your goal. When you finally achieve your goals and look back on how much you have grown, you will realize that you would have not wanted it any other way.

The underlying lessons taught in this text apply to all areas of life, but learning them through the route of attracting women provides a path with great motivation, rewards, and instant feedback. Additionally, by working on an area of life that many find to be their most hopeless, the improvements you make will be more impactful. You will be amazed when you see how your confidence and success in this particular domain will spill over into multiple areas of your life. By choosing to make yourself more attractive to women, you are simultaneously choosing to become a better man.

Chapter 2: Healthy Entitlement and Limiting Beliefs

"Whether you think you can, or you think you can't
— you're right."
-Henry Ford

Entitlement, self-esteem and the belief of one's self-worth are notions that are woven deep into the fabric of a person. Every person's own personal history and life experiences lead them to having unique beliefs about themselves and others. The subject of entitlement must be approached carefully, since it is easy to misconstrue what I write if you are only identifying the word "entitlement" with its negative connotations.

Entitlement is purely a mental construct. It is either a belief in your own mind or a judgment made in the minds of others. Either way, entitlement is not a tangible element that can actually be measured. If you feel entitled, then you are entitled. Some people feel entitled because they were born into an affluent position in their society. Others have worked incredible hard to achieve something, and thus feel entitled to the fruits of their labor. Some people are just incredibly conceited and think that the world owes them everything. In reality, we are all the same. The world was here first and it owes each of us nothing.

Our sense of entitlement stems from our beliefs about ourselves and our role in a particular environment or the world in general. Ask yourself from where you derive your own sense of entitlement or self-worth? For many men, it either comes from their career, good grades, social status, relationships or wealth. Thus their feeling of entitlement is conditional on external sources and would quickly vanish if their external situations were to change. This does not mean that one should not strive to achieve external success, only that one's sense of entitlement should not be attached solely to it. One should instead draw their sense of entitlement from inside themselves through the realization that all people have the same intrinsic value.

Many times your sense of entitlement is situational and tied to what you perceive your level of authority to be in a given environment. If you are a senior physician at a hospital, it is only logical for the less experienced interns to defer to you. However, outside of professional environments, one's entitlement is much more subjective and often is completely gauged off their behavior. When you are participating in a meeting in which you are an expert of the topic under discussion, you probably grant yourself the liberty to speak freely, confidently and do not greatly worry about the opinions that others have of you.

If you then leave work and transition to a cocktail party populated by strangers who are employed in different professions, your confidence may instantly dissolve. While your sense of authority and expertise may change based on a situation or environment, your sense of self-worth should remain the same. Having a high sense of self-worth allows one to engage in different situations and environments without losing the feeling that they have value as well as can provide value to others.

In regards to relationships, a healthy sense of entitlement is feeling that there is no reason that you are not good enough to be with another person. This is different from an unhealthy sense of entitlement which tells you that you deserve to be with another person. Some men who feel jilted by women can come from a dark place where they feel entitled that women should like them. Many of these men have bought heavily into the mainstream fallacies regarding attraction and are incredibly frustrated by their results. They feel that they are "good guys" and have "done everything that society told them they should to do," and believe women should like them for it. They then further use the mainstream model to rationalize their failure as being because they are not rich, popular or good looking enough.

Firstly, you don't deserve to be rewarded for doing what you know is right, or for being a good person. If you are only doing a good deed to get something in return, then it is not really a good deed. Secondly, you must take full responsibility for your actions and the results they have yielded thus far. If you continue to identify as a victim, you will never start performing the actions necessary which will lead to success. By identifying as a victim in a no-win situation, you free yourself from taking responsibility for losing. The outright truth is that neither wealth, status, knowledge nor anything else gives one person entitlement to another person.

When men with this unhealthy entitlement approach a woman, they do not act with the same behaviors of a confident man who has a healthy sense of entitlement. It is usually abundantly clear that these men do not feel that they are good enough. Due to feeling inferior, they try to impress or knock a woman off her pedestal. They often search for reasons that they can use to justify feeling superior to a woman, such as having greater wealth or education. They then try to convince a woman that this makes them better than she is. What these men fail to realize is that they are often the ones who have placed a woman on a pedestal in the first place.

If you find yourself angry or under personal attack after reading these last few paragraphs on unhealthy entitlement, then you probably have it to some degree. You may feel inclined to throw down this book and try to dismiss and forget as quickly as possible what you have just read. As discussed in the previous chapter, this is due to having your current worldview around which you have built your identity under attack. It is your choice to decide to fight these negative thoughts and open your mind to the new paradigm that is being presented to you.

Your actions often mirror your sense of entitlement. When you feel entitled, you are more likely going to act with confidence and assurance. It is ridiculous how far simply having a sense of entitlement can get you. Often you can just do something with no questions asked if you do it with confidence.

Frank Abagnale Jr. was a con man who in the 1960's successfully impersonated being an airline pilot in order to hitch free flights; collectively flying over one million miles around the world. Using fake credentials, he also spent time employed as a physician, college professor and attorney. After one of his multiple arrests, he was even allowed to walk free from prison after being able to convince the prison guards that he was an undercover inspector. Frank was able to pull off all these incredible stunts because of the air of confidence and entitlement that he embodied. I will safely infer that this is also the reason why he was known to be successful with women.

A woman will be more likely to accept an advance from you if it is well calibrated and done with confidence. If you are hesitant or roundabout when asking a woman for her number, then you are communicating to the woman that you are unsure if you are good enough for her. Since actions speak louder than words, a woman will defer to the message that you are sub-communicating. Your personal doubts compounding with a woman's own uncertainty will make her less inclined to want to meet with you.

Alternatively, if you are confident about your actions, a woman is more likely to trust them. There is a big difference between a man who asks a woman out by saying: "If you would be interested in… that is if you are not busy or already have plans… there is a concert Saturday night. I'm not sure if you would like the music… but anyway… would you be interested in maybe going with me?" And a man who straightforwardly says: "I would enjoy getting to know you better. I am going to a concert on Saturday and would love it if you were to join me." The man who projects confidence by assuming that the woman would be interested in joining him is going to be more successful.

To gain a sense of healthy entitlement, one needs to realize that we are all equal and cut from the same cloth. Sure, we all come from different backgrounds, cultures, families, and economic conditions, but it is our choice to let that define our belief that we are of less worth than another person. You can further grow your sense of entitlement through the process of self-development and becoming the man that you truly want to be.

We will now address the primary obstacle which holds a person back from achieving any goal in life, let alone success with women. This is that the person lacks the belief that their goal is actually attainable. Even more debilitating is when one is not even aware that a certain possibility exists. This is one of the reasons (not to belittle the other clear economic reasons) why people born into poverty are likely to remain poor. These individuals grow up in environments which show them little hope for the future and which lack successful role models. In their minds, these individuals think: "What is the purpose of even trying to better myself when in the end I will never succeed?" Likewise, if you are in the typical technical environment, then you may also lack both hope and role models for becoming successful with women.

If you do not have full belief in a system, then you will never invest in it enough to get a significant return. Many men believe that having certain looks and material wealth are prerequisites to women being attracted to them. These men spend their free time only focusing on those two areas of their lives, instead of tackling the primary issue straight on. If your target issue is your lack of success with women, then your main goal should be to improve your competency with women, not adding extra pounds of muscle or zeros to your paycheck.

There are three mental steps that one must take before any goal can be brought to fruition.

1. Belief that something is possible.

If you truly believe that something is not possible, then it would be insane to take an action which has a one hundred percent chance of failure. However, almost nothing in life has a one hundred percent guarantee of either success or failure. Before embarking on a goal, you do not need to be sure that you will be successful (and you often won't), but you should be certain that success is at least a possible outcome.

Fortunately, when it comes to attracting women, there is a 100% guarantee that you will improve if you put in the work. So you have no excuses! The first mental hurdle to overcome is to truly believe that this is the case. If you never venture outside your normal environment, then you may have no reference points to confirm this. This was the case for me while I was still in university. If this is also the case for you, then let the following story serve as confirmation.

During university, I spent every day with a group of likeminded students who like me never met any women. That was until one day I was assigned a lab partner named Jeff. Jeff was not your typical physics student. Jeff was naturally brilliant, but also naturally good with women. I started going out to bars with Jeff in the evening and watching him in action. Jeff was perhaps a bit better looking than me, but his hygiene was usually lacking. He often had not showered in days, had bedhead hair, and wore a ripped and stained pullover sweatshirt; basically the standard uniform worn by most undergraduate engineering students.

However, Jeff would consistently be picking up and bring girls home. On one particular night, he left with a girl that he had just met after only five minutes of conversation. This served as a wakeup call to me. Clearly there was something taking place that I did not yet see or understand. How did speaking to a girl about seemingly nothing for only a few minutes illicit such a response? I now know that it was due to his positive energy, being nonjudgmental and having freedom from outcome, but at the time I was dumbstruck. However, from then on it was clear to me that such things were at least possible.

2. Belief that something is possible for you.

The next step is to believe that you personally are capable of achieving your goal. Perhaps you think that you lack the necessary traits to be successful with women. You tell yourself that: "yes, it is possible for others, but not for me. I am too shy, too short, or too poor for girls to ever like me." These are not only excuses, but they are also not even the primary factors that generate attraction in a woman. Anyone can become better with women if they put in the effort. Many people choose to believe that something is not possible for them, because if they were to accept that it was possible, then they would also have to accept that they were too much of a coward to take action. They would have to accept that their lives could have been drastically different, had they made the choice to change them. They would have to stop blaming external circumstances and start taking responsibility for their life.

3. Choosing to take action and work towards turning a possibility into a reality.

After you believe that you can accomplish your goal, the final hurdle is to overcome procrastination. This procrastination is fueled by a combination of fear and laziness. You tell yourself that someday you will start working towards your goal, but not today. You are afraid to even take the first step. Perhaps you muster up the courage and do take the first step, but it is met with a hostile response which frightens you from ever trying again. Being able to persist through adversity is what truly separates the men from the boys.

You should learn to embrace fear, and use it as a compass. Usually the things that we put off the most are the things that most need to be done. Instead of fearing the consequences of taking an action, fear the consequences of not taking that action. The overall pain in the long term is likely way worse than any immediate discomfort. Would you rather get a vaccination shot now or later become crippled by a preventable disease? You can learn to love the struggle and have pride in yourself for having the courage to work at making yourself a better person. As you begin to amount small successes, you will start a powerful positive feedback loop which will reinforce your belief in yourself and push you to take even greater action.

There will be many barriers to overcome on your journey of self-improvement. You may be surprised to find that lifelong friends may ridicule you and try to hold you back. There are multiple reasons why they may try to do this. Firstly, they may care about you and are afraid to see you get hurt if you fail, or may even fear your success because it means that they might lose you from their lives. Another reason is that they may not want their comfortable reality challenged, and your actions make them reflect on their own lives. If you can succeed, then they must consider what this means for them. Rather than serving as an inspiration, you can serve as a reminder of what they too could have achieved if they had chosen to put in the effort.

Sadly, some people will actually hate you for your new success and confidence because it reminds them of their own low self-esteem, which now in comparison to yours seems even lower. Try to identify the reasons behind people's actions before you judge them. In addition, be aware of becoming resentful of your complacent friends who may serve as constant reminders of what you are fighting so hard to escape. As stated by Robert Pirsig:

> *"We always condemn most in others, that which we most fear in ourselves."*

The greatest success barriers will likely come from within you. It is common to commit self-sabotage because success leads to change and change can be scary. This often takes place on a subconscious level, where your brain will rationalize a decision before you can even consciously question it. It is more comfortable to remain in a known space than venture into the unknown. Your fear of change may cause you to rationalize your limiting beliefs in order to protect yourself and justify inaction.

You may believe that if you were to try and fail, then you would only prove to yourself without a doubt that you are not good enough. Thus you put off trying in order to preserve hope and protect the belief that you will succeed in the future. You must remind yourself that failing does not equate to failure. As long as you keep honestly trying and learning from your mistakes, then you have no other option but to improve. The only true failure is outright choosing inaction.

Our belief systems govern how we act. Your personal system of beliefs and sense of identity has been shaped since the day you were born from external input and feedback. By the time you leave adolescence, you have a solid notion of your place in the world. Even if you are not happy where you are, subconsciously your brain wants to preserve this identity because thus far it has been sufficient for your survival. Any change from the status quo could pose a threat. Your brain's default setting is set to surviving not thriving.

This is why we are constantly seeking validation for our current beliefs, while subconsciously tuning out or rationalizing away the things which don't fit into our world model. This behavior only leads to self-fulfilling prophecies in which we can tell ourselves: "I told you so." A person who holds the belief that all people are selfish assholes often acts in a way that provokes others to treat him negatively, thus forcing these people to live up to his expectations. Similarly, a man who believes that all women are cheating sluts will spend time with the type of women which confirm his suspicions.

In psychology this is known as a confirmation bias: where you favor information that confirms your beliefs while more easily dismissing possible alternatives. Rather than having their beliefs challenged, some people choose to dig in so deep with their current views that any contradictory voices can no longer be heard, including the small voice inside them.

You attract what you are, and bring into your life only what you think you deserve. If you are a damaged person, then you are more likely to invite other damaged individuals into your life who serve to fortify your belief system. If you are learning this material for the sole reason of wanting validation from women, then the women that you attract will also trend towards those who use men as a source of validation.

When a man and a woman who are both craving validation meet, their combined insecurities lead to the playing of unnecessary and time consuming games. A push-pull dynamic will often be established where they are constantly rewarding and punishing one another through the providing and withholding of validation. For example, if one of them does not return a text message quick enough, the other person reacts by unnecessarily delaying their reply. Another example is when one person responds to feeling jealous by purposefully trying to incite jealousy in the other person. By fully approving of yourself and finding a woman who is also self-secure, you can instead create a healthy relationship where neither of you requires constant validation from the other.

Many believe that they need to become what society or others have defined as suitable to be worthy of affection. They realize that whenever they perform such-and-such a behavior or live up to some standard, they are rewarded by being accepted. However, they are living their lives by an arbitrary set of rules determined by others. They are provided a small reward of temporary acceptance in return for sacrificing their true identity. This negative feedback loop can be broken by choosing to have personal integrity and living a life which is in line with one's own chosen beliefs, not the beliefs imposed on one by others.

Chapter 3: Scarcity Mindset vs. Abundance Mindset

"Instead, I have an abundance mentality: When people are genuinely happy at the successes of others, the pie gets larger."
-Stephen Covey

I have found the principle of scarcity to be the most influential factor that affects how a man interacts with a woman. Many major life decisions, often on an unconscious level, are decided based upon one's beliefs regarding scarcity. Scarcity causes us to make fear based decisions while rationalizing our choices to settle for less than what we truly desire. Scarcity causes us to work jobs that we don't like, remain associated with people who bring us down and marry those that we do not truly love.

The primary payoff from becoming successful with women is not actually the act of being with many women, but the freedom from scarcity that results from it. You will regain clear control over your decision making ability, while freeing yourself from the crushing fear of being alone. Many men severely compromise their lifestyles, social lives, finances and personal freedom as a result of the decisions they make while operating in a scarcity mindset.

We have all witnessed the devastating aftermath that can result from making scarcity based decisions. It is not uncommon to watch a man go broke while trying to buy the love of a woman. During the Cold War, an American CIA official became a double agent for the Soviet Union in return for large sums of money. His motivation was to please his newly married Columbian wife who had expensive taste. Upon being discovered as a mole, both he and his new wife were sent to prison. In this extreme case, a scarcity mentality contributed to a man becoming a traitor to his own country.

Scarcity mentalities create couples who openly despise one another, yet remain together because of their mutual fear of having to meet new people. A scarcity mentality also causes a woman to repeatedly return back to the man who abuses her, believing that she does not deserve anything better. Beliefs regarding scarcity can cloud a person's judgment and keep them rationalizing their destructive choices. Over time this can tear apart a person's finances, relationships and physical health.

Scarcity is linked to what we perceive as being available to us. Thus if you have a scarcity of women in your life, then this is going to drastically affect your behavior. You are going to become needy and desperate around the few women of whom you find desirable. You will be worried that they may be one of your only few chances at finding love or a mate, and thus your actions will be fueled by fear and anxiety. While in a relationship, scarcity can cause one to be overprotective, jealous and controlling. You may also be willing to overlook the terrible personality flaws that a person may have, and attach yourself to a ticking time bomb.

Your desperation will prevent you from succeeding with women which in turn will only further plunge you into a scarcity mindset. It can be a vicious downward cycle. You may become paralyzed by the fear of ever asking a particular woman out, since you may interpret a rejection from her as you losing your one shot at love. By keeping the situation ambiguous, you can at least take refuge and find comfort in your self-delusional fantasy that one day you could potentially be together.

Most young males operating in a scarcity mindset catch the disease *Oneitis* at some point in their young adult lives. If not promptly caught and cured, *Oneitis* can take years away from one's life. You can pour all your time and energy into a lost cause instead of using it to improve yourself. Having suffered myself from a very dire case of the disease, I am accustomed to the symptoms. The symptoms of *Oneitis* can include:

- Spending an abnormal amount of time thinking and obsessing over one girl.
- Believing that one girl is completely different from every other girl that you have ever met.
- Believing that one girl is the most beautiful girl in the world.
- Believing that there is no other girl for you but her.
- Believing that no one else could ever match the love that you have for a girl.
- Believing that a girl is absolutely perfect and could do no wrong in your eyes.
- Putting a girl before everything else in your life.

An additional symptom would include not seeing anything wrong with holding the above beliefs. You may believe that if a girl only truly knew how much you cared about her, that she would love you in return. However, this is not the way attraction or love actually works. When you truly love a person, you do not need anything from them in return. Arriving at this realization took me years and was the most painful lesson that I have ever had to learn. There is no such thing as "the one," but only people who are more or less compatible together. Love is something you build, not something you find.

While I have no doubt that the feelings which you have are genuine, these feelings originate from a place of scarcity and fear. You may mistake the burning desire you have for a woman as the being the truest form of love. Fear resulting from scarcity infiltrates the heart and amplifies certain emotions to an unhealthy level. If this is the first time that you have ever felt this way, then you may be terrified of losing the woman for whom you feel these feelings. You may fear that you may never again feel this same way about anyone else. The truth is that you may be right. However, this is not due to you having lost out on the love of your life, but to the fact that you no longer live in scarcity. Once the scarcity mindset is removed, you can find someone with whom you can have a relationship with that is built on positive emotions, instead of the hidden underlying emotions of loneliness and fear.

Now looking back, having my heart broken was one of the best things that could have ever happened to me. Had a need based relationship instead ensued, I would have never become the person I am today. I would have unknowingly submitted to comfort and security rather than venturing out into the world to learn its truths for myself. I would have remained a weak man and never developed the deep self-love, self-confidence and self-reliance which are prerequisites to unselfishly loving another person.

Although at first it may sound incredibly counterintuitive, but a woman does not actually want you to put her before everything else in your life. A woman does not want you to be completely dependent on her for your own happiness. For a healthy relationship to exist, the center of your life needs to be your own personal purpose, not a need to please another person. While this may sound selfish, it is much more selfish to take the responsibility of your own personal happiness off yourself and force it on a woman. A woman would much rather be invited along on your amazing life journey than have you hitch yourself to her life.

Giving up your own career, friends, hobbies and interests all in an attempt to please a woman will never yield positive results. While all relationships require compromises to be made by both parties, healthy compromises are made for the long term mutual benefit of a couple as a whole. These are different than one-sided compromises which are motivated solely by the desire to receive affection. Not only can you not buy true affection in this way, but such actions are actually completely counterproductive. A woman does not want a man who is so easily willing to sacrifice his own personal integrity; even if it is being done in her name.

You may be reading this book because you desire the affection of one specific woman. However, if you are only after one specific woman, then you have already placed yourself in scarcity. Acting from a place of scarcity is going to incredible lower your chances of being successful with this woman. Neediness is the prime killer of attraction. A woman knows that a man who cannot provide for his own emotional wellbeing will not be able to contribute to hers. You must first focus on getting good with women in general before you can have choices in the matter.

If you currently have a case of *Oneitis*, your natural instinct may be to dismiss what you have just read. However, you can save yourself from a lot of pain and lost time by forcing yourself to start facing the facts. Otherwise, your *Oneitis* fever is finally going to break one evening when you invite your love over to your house for a party and she proceeds to hookup in your bedroom with a guy that she just met. During those moments in life when you feel that your entire world is coming crashing down, you will have a critical choice to make. You can choose to either double down on your false beliefs or take the massive action required to shift your paradigm.

Tony Robbins says that "in life you need either inspiration or desperation." The pain you feel from heartbreak, rejection or loneliness can either be wallowed in or used constructively to make you stronger and to provide motivation. What may begin as a journey initiated from a place of pain, will hopefully end in a place of inspiration. You will be inspired as you witness yourself accomplish things which you never before imagined possible. When a great woman then comes along, you will have the best chance with her, since you will be coming from a place of abundance.

The catch-22 of this situation is that it is easy to act with the confidence required to attract women when you are in abundance. But how do you initially obtain this confidence when you currently lack even a single woman in your life? Confidence is created by having successful past reference experiences to draw from. If you have beaten almost everyone you know at chess, then you probably are confident about winning a game against a new opponent.

Imagine that you have dated multiple supermodels in the past (ok that's enough, quit imagining and keep reading), with those reference experiences you would have the confidence to believe that you are worthy of dating other girls of similar looks and status in the future. You may have noticed that more girls seem interested in you when you have a girlfriend. This is because you are coming off as being non-needy and not currently operating in a scarcity mindset. The rich get richer since they can act confidently from a position of abundance.

If you are starting from scratch, then you need to slowly start building positive reference experiences and buy into the paradigm described in this book. As success results from applying the principles described in later chapters, it will become easier to fully accept the model for attraction presented. Thus while you may not yet be able to derive confidence from a plethora of positive experiences, you can derive confidence from knowing that the application of these principles will eventually lead you to the success that you desire. Don't expect your results to be instantaneous, just as you would not expect to see results after spending just one day at the gym. There will be many high, lows and plateaus along the way.

Take a moment to reflect and analyze how scarcity may be affecting you. If you spend the majority of your time either in a cubicle at work or on your couch at home, it should be no surprise that you may have conditioned yourself into a scarcity mindset. Your current lifestyle may lack even potential opportunities to meet new women. If you know that you will only be introduced to a few new women a year, then you will never be able to shake off the destructive power that scarcity holds over you.

Scarcity also potentially puts more pressure on women than on men. As many women near their thirties and feel their childbearing years ticking away, they often start to become desperate to find a mate and settle down. Many of these women will then make the decision to marry a less ideal man rather than remain childless. She may even later hold resentment towards this man for not being the man that she wishes him to truly be. Do you really want to be in a relationship where you know in the back of your mind that at least one of you is settling for the other? A woman wants a man who chooses her over other options.

This is the classic Prince Charming fantasy brought to life: where the prince chooses a plain woman from among many admirers because he discovers something special about her. The prince in the story does not go around slaying dragons for the sole purpose of trying to impress the ladies and earn their approval. He does it because he is a natural badass who is pursuing his purpose and taking care of business along the way.

When one lives life with an abundance mentality, they do not fear temporary failure or loss because another opportunity is always around the corner. This belief provides one with a powerful outlook and causes almost all the other traits of an attractive man to naturally present themselves. When it comes to negotiating, the person who cares the most often loses. Being able to walk away from a woman, while holding the belief that you can meet someone else, automatically puts the cards in your favor by signaling that you have options. When a woman senses this, she knows that you value yourself more than her approval, and she will find this attractive.

Women are attracted to self-sufficient men who do not come off as being needy. This is a reason among others why some women are attracted to men who don't seem to care about them at all. If you know that you can currently choose from a large pool of women to date, it is easy to be outcome independent when interacting with one specific woman. Being not dependent on an interaction's outcome in turn removes one's fear of rejection. The removal of fear then results in one presenting themselves at their best and greatly increases their chance of being successful. Any resulting success only then adds to one's feeling of abundance, and one enters a positive upward cycle.

After arriving back from a month long trip, I showed to a friend a picture of an extraordinarily beautiful girl that I had dated during the time I was away. He was shocked by her beauty and asked me why I decided not to continue my relationship with her even over long distance. He himself had a girlfriend who he rarely saw because she lived in another country. He told me — only half-jokingly — that I should have proposed to her before leaving.

My friend was clearly coming from a scarcity mindset. To him I had won the lottery and then decided not to cash in my ticket. While I indeed had met an extraordinarily beautiful and kind woman, I was not going to restructure my whole life due to a three week relationship. I was able to enjoy the time I had with this woman, while remaining confident that I could again meet another woman of equal caliber in the future.

True abundance is having the belief that you possess the skills to obtain something even if you lose everything that you currently have. This belief is what allows one to successfully navigate through hard times. It is what enables an entrepreneur to remake his fortune after completely losing all his original wealth. It is what empowers a star NBA player bring a game back from the brink of defeat. It is what allows a politician to lose a local election only to become the President of the United States years later. You know since you have done something before that you can do it again, which lets you act with confidence even if you currently have nothing to show.

Being in abundance allows you to set personal boundaries and filter out the people who cross them without fearing being alone. As a result, you will start filling your life with higher quality individuals and healthier relationships. The removal of neediness takes a huge uncomfortable pressure out of interactions. When you are in abundance, and thus not seeking value from those around you, it results in the formation of deeper and truer relationships.

When it comes to attracting women, scarcity exists in two separate forms: physical and mental. We have just talked about the how the scarcity mentality may be preventing you from believing that you have options. Furthermore, the physical environment in which you reside may also be preventing you from meeting women. This is typically the situation for those studying or working in technical professions. The solution to overcome the physical scarcity of women in one's environment is simple. Spend your time in new environments! In comparison, overcoming mental scarcity will take much more work than simply deciding to take one's lunch break at the vegan restaurant next to the yoga studio rather than at your desk.

The flake equation is a useful tool for showing how crucial one's environment is for meeting women. The flake equation allows one to roughly estimate the number of women that will go out with (not flake on) them.

$$N = W \cdot f_d \cdot f_i \cdot G \cdot f_a \cdot f_l$$

N= Number of dates

The first four variables of the equation can directly be manipulated and improved in your favor by taking the proper actions. The final two variables of the equation you have no control over.

Controllable Variables

W= Physical number of women in your environment

Many men overlook the simple fact that they spend their entire days within women deficient environments. Do you wonder why you never meet any girls? Well how many women do you even observe in a single day? Given the low probability that the university's entire cheerleading team is going to enroll in your thermodynamics lecture next semester, perhaps you should place yourself into some new environments. This might take some effort if your entire 9-5 existence takes place in a cubicle on the 4th floor of a celibate man zoo. Pining over the one girl in your engineering lecture or the office secretary is a complete waste of time. You should first concentrate on getting good with women in general before you focus on a single one.

f_d= Fraction of these women that you find desirable

Hopefully you have selected women rich environments to actively frequent which contain women that you find desirable. An environment will have a large influence on the average age, education level, personality type, and physical fitness of the individuals present. You might get a lot of attention at the senior citizen center, but it's probably not the kind that you are particularly looking for. It takes relatively little effort to place yourself for at least one hour a day in a place which contains women that you find attractive.

f_i= Fraction of these women with which you interact

So now that you have placed yourself in the right environment, you now must interact with these women. You will have to get over your approach anxiety. For many people, learning to engage strangers can be extremely difficult. No amount of theory can take the place of experience.

G= Personal Game constant $0 \leq G \geq 1$

Your personal game constant is the combination of your attraction skill set and overall desirability. By learning from past interactions, you can improve your game constant. Having a theoretical game constant of 1 would result in every woman you interacted with becoming attracted to you. While theoretically possible, a perfect game constant does not actually exist in nature. Every woman has her own taste in men, and it is perfectly normal that not everyone is compatible. To force compatibility would require you to be manipulative and disingenuous to both the woman and yourself.

Uncontrollable Variables

f_a= Fraction of these woman that are available

A faction of these women will already be in relationships. While they may become attracted to you, they will likely not act on that attraction.

f_l= Fraction of these women not blocked by logistics

The logistical situation involving a girl's friends, family approval, religion, social image, living situation and countless other unforeseen variables will always be present.

The truth is that at some level this is a numbers game. If you are reading this from the inside of a prison (the engineering quad is not an actual prison since you can legally leave), then there is nothing that can be done. Otherwise, you are making the choice to spend your time in environments that are not conducive to meeting women. You would not expect to meet a penguin in the Sahara desert, thus likewise do not expect to meet desirable women at a LAN party. You may need to expand your comfort zone and place yourself in environments that may be new to you such as parks, bars and coffee shops. As your social skills improve along with your time spent in non-scare environments, regularly meeting great women will just seem to be an innate part of your life.

Chapter 4: Windows BC:
An Outdated Operating System

"Attraction is not a choice."

Humans (Homo Sapiens) first emerged on Earth roughly 200,000 years ago. Before developing agriculture, we roamed the land in small tribes of hunters and gatherers. Our brains today still contain much of the original hardwiring left over from nearly a quarter million years ago. In the not so distant past, human communities only roughly contained around 150 individuals. The modern metropolises that we have today have only emerged in the last few hundred years. While our environments have drastically changed, the software running in our minds has primarily remained the same. While there is of course more at play in modern day romance than old evolutionary impulses alone, it would be ignorant to believe that past evolutionary forces are not still at work.

The first outdated software thread that we need to patch is our fear of rejection. Imagine that you are in a coffee shop while vacationing in a city far from home. As you are paying for your beverage, you spot a beautiful woman who is sitting alone reading a book. You have the initial desire to start a conversation with her, and start walking in her direction. However, within seconds you start to feel nervous as fears and doubts begin to infiltrate your mind. After you have closed half the distance to her, the woman gazes up from her book and locks eyes with you. Using her hand, she combs her hair back behind her ear and gives you a small smile. At this point your heart starts pounding faster in your chest. Your mind goes blank with the words you were going to say as your knees begin to slightly shake. She is only five feet from you now; four, three, two, one. The bell in the upper corner of the door rings as you decide to walk past her and out into the street.

Can you think of any rational reason why you should have feared saying "hello" to this woman? You will never see her again and there was no one else around to even judge you. While in hindsight your fear seems ridiculous, the outdated firmware running in your brain was doing its best to protect you. Had this same situation occurred 10,000 years ago at a watering hole in the Neolithic era, your very life may have been at risk. In a tribe of only 150 people, females of reproductive age would be highly coveted. Had this woman already belonged to the tribal leader, he may have taken your advance as a threat and then promptly smashed a rock into your skull. Fortunately in modern day society, the threat of taking a rock to the head is not one you should likely concern yourself with while waiting in line at a Jamba Juice.

Other than being the recipient of bodily harm, your fear also stems from the consequences of social ostracism. If you interact with this woman, you could come off looking like a fool. This one woman could then gossip about you to all the other women in your tribe while they are all out together picking berries. Thus your advance could have resulted in you committing social suicide. All the women in the tribe would have a preconceived view of you as a loser and none would want to risk their reputation by associating with you. Even worse you could be cast out of the tribe and left to fend for yourself.

While the tribal leader Chad might have been a bit of a dick who kept all the women for himself, at least he brought protection to your group and let you eat from the scraps of his kill. Now that you are left out on your own, you have a small chance of surviving. Most other tribes would not accept you and may try to kill you, and alone you are just a sitting duck for a hungry tiger.

Both death and social ostracism would bring your genetic lineage to an end. Your genes do not want what is best for you as a whole; they want what is best for them. In some degree, your person is just the vehicle through which your genes try to reach a future generation. Thousands of years of evolution have hammered these notions and fears into your head. While you can try to rationalize that these facts are no longer the case, your brain still wants hard evidence. You must provide your brain with the proof it desires through the gaining of reference experiences in which you interact with women and then proceed not to die.

Your high school class, college campus or office may represent a modern day tribe. In these environments your social reputation is somewhat at stake. Thus if you are completely inept at social interaction, it would be better to practice somewhere that you have anonymity. Living in a large city or traveling to new places is the best way to accomplish this.

Just as men are biologically attracted to women that have forms which display positive reproductive qualities, women are also attracted to specific characteristics in men. Fortunately for men, the vast majority of women do not put nearly the same importance on physical appearance as men do. Attraction is not a choice, however choosing to act on it is. Men find women with a certain hip to waist ratio attractive since it signals a high probability of there being smooth sailing when it comes time to give birth. Thus a certain hip to waist ratio translates into a higher chance of survival for both the child and the mother. Likewise, women also look for traits in men which signal to them that their offspring will have an increased chance of survival.

When looking at a man's traits from this prospective, it should not be surprising that physical attractiveness would not top the list. While looking healthy and being physically fit is important; how would a man having perfect facial symmetry really benefit a woman? Facial symmetry will not make a man a better provider or protector. Having a strong jaw line is not going to stop a horde of barbarians from pillaging your hut and stealing your wife. While the passing on of physical attractiveness genes to one's offspring is important, these genes can primarily come from the woman alone.

The first signals that women look for in a man are pre-selection and social proof. A woman views a man as being pre-selected when she witnesses other women expressing interest in him. The concept of social proof extends past pre-selection to include all endorsements a person directly and indirectly receives from others. For example, if a woman does not know a man, but sees him engaging positively with other individuals who she knows to be well-respected, then through association she may automatically think more highly of him. Likewise, if everyone seems to know a man and hold him in high regard, their approval contributes to the woman's perceived value of the man.

Whenever I went out dancing with an extremely attractive female friend, other woman could not take their eyes off me. Starting random conversation with any of these women was incredibly easy, since they would be immediately open and warm towards me. On nights when I would visit the same venue alone, much more effort was required on my part to successfully engage the women present.

On one occasion, I approached a woman there and asked her to dance with me. Her immediate response was to decline. A moment later, my attractive friend came over to inform me that she was going to step outside for a minute. The three seconds of social proof provided to me by my attractive friend, were enough to cause the other woman to reverse her position and want to dance.

When in social engagements, it is always better for a woman to view you as holding a prominent role. I have been at social gatherings, where for the initial few hours I rarely spoke directly to a woman who was present. During this time, I was always addressing other individuals or the group at large. Women at these events became attracted to me from just witnessing my ability to command the group's attention and earn their admiration and approval. Furthermore, since I was not directly interacting with these women, they were less inclined to view my words as an attempt to impress them and thus were more prone to interpret what I was saying as being honest. By the end of these evenings, I only needed to directly acknowledge these women with a simple "hello" for them to melt.

When entering a new environment where no one knows you, you will have to build social proof from scratch. Many men have trouble doing this and thus choose to stick to environments where they are already known and thus feel entitled. I have met multiple men, who could have any woman in a salsa club, be unable to speak to women elsewhere. Wealthy men often try to purchase social proof by ordering expensive bottle service at a club or even by paying attractive escorts to stand next to them.

For me personally, the best part of developing one's social skills is gaining the ability to bring new people into your life. By learning how to effectively communicate, I can now travel alone to a new country and within a week make local friends and have amazing experiences. I can create opportunities on my own instead of being dependent on my external environment to provide them.

Pre-selection can save a woman both time and energy when looking for a mate. If a man is already surrounded by other women, especially ones that are signaling interest in him, then these other women have most likely already screened the man for having attractive traits. Women will naturally be curious about what makes this particular man so special, and be less concerned about the man potentially being a bad choice. They think to themselves: "If he is good enough that all these other women to have chosen him, then he is also likely a safe choice for me."

Women often go for guys that are labeled as being "players" because of the fact that these men have been selected by many other women in the past. A common misconception that many men have is thinking that letting a woman know you have been spending time with other women will be a turnoff to her. The opposite is usually true, where the social proof that you receive from having other women in your life will in turn make a woman more interested in you. Some women even take this to the extreme and go specifically for men who are either in relationships or married.

This is not to say that one should be cheating and seeing other women while in a relationship. That will definitely be a turnoff to most women. But a woman knowing that you would be able to quickly meet another high quality woman following the end of a current relationship will not be a turn off. While a woman being surrounded by men normally causes a man to rationalize away his interest, a man surrounded by women will only heighten the interest of other women.

Pre-selection leads to a woman presupposing that a man possesses other attractive traits, making it initially the most powerful signal. Pay attention to advertising and you will see how the concepts of pre-selection and social proof are used by marketers to sell products. People often buy a product because of celebrity endorsements or since all of their friends are already using it. Rather than risking choosing an inferior product, people often instead go with what they know.

The position of leader almost always carries with it a degree of social proof. Women are attracted to a man who is a leader and is not afraid to step up and take charge of a situation. Being a leader conveys high social status, power and that you have the capability to solve problems. Women find a man highly attractive when they witness other men give him respect and defer decisions to him. Leaders are often also socially savvy and know how to properly behave in most situations. In past societies, tribal leaders often took the majority of the women for themselves. While a woman might not like the idea of sharing the leader with other women, many would prefer it over being with a man who could not provide at all for her. In many ways, modern day marriage protects lower status men from being left without a mate.

Women want to feel that they are with a man who can protect them. If a guy cannot even stand up for himself, how could he ever protect someone else? It is attractive when a man can fend for himself and deal with life's problems without burdening his woman. In the Neolithic era, a man's physical strength and fitness would directly correlate with his ability to protect a woman. As time went on, a man's social status and access to resources became of increasing importance. In Egypt, the physically strongest men were not the leaders, but those dragging the stones to build the pharaohs' pyramids.

While women are interested in a man who can provide and care for both them and a potential family, in modern Western society this is now less of a concern. Most women in the Western world can easily earn a living on their own or can rely on a government provided social system. Regardless of this fact, many men still believe that wealth is the most important factor to attracting women. Thus predominantly driven by loneliness, these men work themselves into the ground and go into massive debt in the attempt to attract women via material possessions. These fallacies are heavily propagated by our consumer media given that this is one of the strongest motives that they can use to turn a profit from you.

Ironically, if these men used all the hours they spent working overtime to earn money in an attempt to impress women, to instead invest in themselves, they would have more women, time and wealth. Naturally, there are a percentage of women that are overly concerned about status and material wealth. They often can be seen on TV programs featured on the Bravo channel. These women will want you for your money and usually not much else. However, do you really want to be with a woman that you know will leave you if you can no longer provide a luxurious lifestyle or when someone richer comes along?

Women are interested in a man that can provide in multiple ways, not only financially. Having your finances in order is an important aspect of being a man, but it is only one aspect among many. Back in the caveman days, there was no money and most cave real estate was pretty similar. Thus a resource rich man then was one with good social status who could obtain what he needed by his own means or through that of his connections.

Finally, women are attracted to a man who is living a life of purpose and has passion for what he does. This is why some women often go for the broke musician or starving artist. As will be described in detail in a later chapter, when a man expresses passion for something, a woman will feel this same passion within herself. A woman wants a man who is secure with who he is and the type of life he lives. Purpose is the invisible backbone that allows a man to hold himself steady through the currents of life. Women want a man who is driven to accomplish his goals. While most women do not want to be put ahead of everything else in your life, they still want to feel secure that you will not leave them behind as you move forward.

When it comes to relationships, a woman wants a man who will commit to her. However, the woman wants this commitment to be of the man's own choosing and not be a result of his lack of ability to find someone else. A woman must balance her desire between a provider who will stick around and a man who carries good genes; a balance between providing security and having attractive traits. You need to be able to provide for a woman's emotional needs, not only her physical ones. Thus as a man it is better to develop attractive traits and not just rely on being a good provider, especially in modern day society where a woman can provide for herself. Furthermore, you want a woman to actually desire you before she rationalizes what you can provide for her.

The human intellect and language abilities make us much more capable of deception than other members of the animal kingdom. Women are aware that men will often try to present themselves in a way that is inaccurate to how they truly are. Of course women dress and use beauty products to alter their physical appearance, but as men we often find this acceptable. Meanwhile, women will find any type of deception as being completely repugnant.

To screen for the above traits, women will look for honest signals that men give which are difficult to fake. Among the most honest signals are the behavioral cues of being able to comfortably hold eye contact and speak with a steady tone that lacks inflection. Confident behaviors such as these usually result from a man having prior success. A woman subconsciously thinks that for a man to have the confidence that he shows, many other women must have responded positively to his advances in the past. This makes her more intrigued to find out what about the man allows him to act in this way.

Being able to trust that a man is communicating honest signals (both physically and verbally) is of incredible importance to a woman. Women have become incredibly adept at detecting bullshit. Before deciding to be with a man, a woman wants to be sure that a man actually is as he appears to be. Evolutionarily this makes sense, since being deceived could result in a woman stuck raising a child with substandard genes.

In order to be completely honest, it is important to speak one's own mind and not tailor one's beliefs to what you think a woman wants to hear. A woman will appreciate that you are genuine and honest, even if she disagrees with your stance on an issue. Your willingness to actively disagree with her also lets her know that you are not simply altering your beliefs in an attempt to please her. The woman then knows that she can reliably use your words to screen for other attractive traits. A woman does not want to waste her time getting to know someone who is disingenuous. Honest communication is an important facet of attraction that will repeatedly reappear throughout the remainder of this book.

Chapter 5: Relativity, Reference Frames and Alternative Realities

"I reject your reality and substitute my own."
-Popularized by Adam Savage

Every person has a unique perspective formed by their collective memory of past experiences. Our personal histories, parents and the culture that we were born into play a large role in shaping who we are. We will refer to this unique perspective as one's reality or worldview. To make sense of a new event, we reference it against other past events that have taken place in our lives. Consequently, two people may interpret differently the same event due to it being filtered through their individual perspectives. When something is outside of your reality, it can almost never actualize in your life; and for the cases in which it does, you will most likely mistake the reasons why.

If dating great women is completely outside of your reality, then you will never take the actions necessary for it to occur. This directly relates back to the chapter on limiting beliefs. There have likely been multiple opportunities which you have completely missed out on, simply due to them being outside of your reality and thus invisible to you. The limit of your reality may currently reside somewhere in-between being able to start a conversation with an unfamiliar woman, getting her phone number, kissing her within minutes of meeting, to having her take you home.

One evening, a couple years prior to my discovering the principles in this book, a girl invited me to go out dancing with her friends. We spent the evening dancing and ended up kissing. When it got late, the girl told me that she had to walk her friends back home, but that she would come back later and find me. To my slight surprise, two hours later she actually did come back alone. We danced some more before I walked her to the taxi stand. She climbed into the taxi's backseat, scooted over to make room, and gave me a look which said: "Are you coming?" Rather than climbing in after the girl, I instead proceeded to slam the door closed behind her and tap twice on the taxi's roof. It was not until two full seconds later, as I watched the car drive off, that I realized my mistake.

Due to my lack of experience at the time, it was still totally outside my reality that this girl may have wanted me to go home with her. It doesn't take Scooby Doo to put together the clues of a girl inviting me out dancing, kissing me, and then coming back alone to the venue two hours later to find me. While a painful lesson to learn, my personal view of reality expanded that day.

While certain events may blow your reality wide open, broadening one's reality is more often a process of it slowly being stretched wider and wider. As your personal view of reality expands, your mind will scramble to rationalize what you are newly witnessing. The purpose of this book is to provide an accurate model of attraction for your mind to grasp onto when new experiences conflict with your current erroneous worldview.

The human mind primarily classifies objects, people and situations through the drawing of comparisons. We measure wealth, beauty, freedom and happiness in relation to what we have previously witnessed or experienced in our own lives or in the lives of others. We label food as tasting good only in relation to food which we have previously found to taste bad. You may have felt intelligent while in high school, and then later only average while surrounded by university colleagues. The cute girl at your small hometown gym would likely appear less stunning if she was placed in a Victoria's Secret lineup. Most people gauge their financial wealth in relation to those directly around them. Live in the Congo for a month, and you may come back feeling quite rich.

Our views of what we are entitled to are also measured in relation to what we have previously experienced in our lives. If you live somewhere in the Western world, you most likely would be upset if you were to lose electrical power for an entire day. However, if you grew up in a place where the rationing of electricity is the norm, then you probably would not complain as much.

In Germany, students revolted when a yearly $500 administrative fee was instated for studying at a university. Up to that point, attending university in Germany was completely tuition free. Having grown up in this system, the students felt entitled that they should not have to pay at all for their degrees, and were able to get the fee overturned. In the United States, where some students pay upwards of $50,000 a year for tuition, a relatively small additional $500 increase would likely not cause much outrage. American students are used to paying over $500 per semester in book costs alone.

If you are extremely desperate for a girlfriend, then any woman who simple qualifies for that position on a genetic level may seem adequate to you. If you have low self-esteem and no boundaries, then you will be more willing to accept putting up with someone who mistreats you. As you develop a healthier sense of entitlement, you may start adding additional criteria for a partner, such as the woman being physically fit, intelligent, trustworthy, and kind.

The environments that you frequently occupy, and the people with whom you regularly interact, greatly shape who you are as a person. You are often roughly the average of the people with whom you spend the most time. This is true in relation to your physical health, income, ambition and dating life. What you even perceive as possible is usually directly linked to what you have previously observed in your local environment. The further away that your environment and friends are from where you want to be, the greater amount of self-discipline you will need to invoke. I recommend finding individuals who can mentor or push you in the areas of your life in which you desire improvement.

If you have never left your small town, your perception of what your possible options are will be limited. If you are studying engineering or work as a programmer in an office, the number of women you interact with may be incredibly finite. The only women that you may picture yourself ever meeting are the three human resource officers stationed between your cubicle and the coffee machine. You may get an instant crush on any women who is kind enough to acknowledge you. Spending all your time only in these environments is going to generate a scarcity mindset.

Now let's take a moment to look at the world through the eyes of an attractive girl. From the age that an attractive girl begins to mature, her view of reality will often develop differently than that of her peers. She will soon learn that she can use her beauty and flirtation to help her acquire what she desires. In her reality, most people are friendly and nice since they are always going out of their way to help her. She will develop a natural sense of entitlement which will be constantly reinforced by the way other people treat her. Both men and women will go out of their way to please this woman in the hopes of landing in her good favor. For highly attractive woman, receiving free favors and gifts can become the norm.

One night out in Düsseldorf, I hit it off with a beautiful woman who later invited me back to spend the night at her place. While sitting on her couch, I noticed a pile of exotic artifacts in the corner of her room. When I asked her about them, she told me that they were from some guy friend who she had only ever met once, but over the years has continued to send her gifts from places all around the world. The most recent gift was a mask that he acquired while visiting an Inca temple in Peru.

On her birthday, this woman was given two round trip tickets to a Caribbean island, again from another man who she has also never actually dated. While she ended up turning down the tickets, along with their clear implications, many women would have gone ahead and enjoyed a free week on the beach.

What I took away from this experience was not only a glimpse into the reality of an extremely attractive woman, but also an impression of what they desire but most men never offer them. This woman chose me not because I could fly her to a tropical island or provide her with exotic gifts. She liked me because I spoke honesty to her, did not hide my intentions, was unapologetic about finding her attractive and showed a genuine interest in actually getting to know her.

On the subway ride back to her house, this woman kept repeating to me: "Please do not turn out to be a needy guy." Clearly, this woman already had enough men in her life who were continuously harassing her with attempts to buy her affection. The opportunity to spend an evening with a man who was completely honest and upfront with her was a rare experience.

Multiple men every day will directly and indirectly hit on an attractive woman. If this woman was to respond to every suitor, then she would likely be left with no time for herself. Thus she will often ignore or dismiss most men with little afterthought. Men who are of low value to her may not even appear on her radar, and register as the equivalent of being a piece of furniture to avoid while crossing the room. Attractive woman have great abundance when it comes to picking a man. Their problem will be finding a man who appreciates them for more than just their looks.

Just as a person born into wealth may become lazy, so can a woman who has won the physical genetic lottery. A woman may never reach her full potential if she can always fall back on her looks to live a comfortable life. However, physical appearance is incredible hard to maintain given that it deteriorates with age. Thus a woman who does not develop herself in other capacities will often be left with nothing but bitterness later on. While such a woman may be showered with gifts and experiences, it is important to remember that she is fully dependent upon others to get them. She herself could likely not acquire such things by her own accord if they were not provided to her through others. Since her beauty has provided her with intrinsic value, she may have never had to learn how to create value on her own. This is not a good place for a person to be at in life when they are entering their early 30s. These women's blessing could soon become their curses. As a man (or as a woman), if you choose to build your sense of entitlement via personal accomplishment, it will only continue to grow over time. Your value will not depreciate but increase with age and experience.

Most people completely buy into the realities that are directly marketed and sold to them. These marketed realities are often created not for your benefit, but for the benefit of someone else far above you. Your pursuit to acquire material items in an indirect attempt to attract women makes others incredibly rich. The media sells you an image so that you use all your time and resources trying to meet it. You could easily spend your entire life trying to become what others are telling you to be instead of who you truly want to become.

People choose to buy into generic realities because they bring them a sense of order and security. People want a model by which they can live their lives, since such a model relieves them from the work and uncertainty that comes with trying to develop their own. Many of those who attempt to disrupt the current order find out that there can be hell to pay for doing so. These people are attacked because they challenge the social narrative which gives others a sense of comfort and security.

Society gives permission for some people to act in certain ways, while simultaneously forbidding the exact same behaviors from others. A woman who may respond positively to derogatory lines spoken to her by a celebrity rap artist, would likely slap you if you were to say them (not that you would actually want to say them). The rapper's image and status allows him to get away with saying certain things that you cannot, since these remarks would be congruent to his character. Society gives handsome and wealthy athletes permission to date the most beautiful women, while telling the remainder of men to just be patient and wait until love comes and finds them.

If you have already been typecast as a nerdy engineer type who is unworthy of the attention of certain women, then even your attempt to court these women may come as an attack on their and other's worldviews. You may be seen as stepping out of line and upsetting society's natural order. You may be berated, punished and shamed for even conceiving that a particular woman could be interested in you.

An example of this would be when a ripped body builder sees women giving more interest to you than to him at the gym. The body builder has fully bought into the world model that being ripped will get you women, and when he sees a relatively scrawny guy killing it with the ladies, his world model is challenged. He has put all this time and effort into his body, and it is not yielding the results with women that he desires. Likewise, you may have put massive amounts of time and energy into building a successful career and have the same issue.

Some people attack success when they see it being achieved via methods that conflict with their own worldviews. They may actively try to thwart any evidence that contradicts with their desired view of reality, rather than face the discomfort of having to question their own long held beliefs. A common scenario is when a so called "nice guy" valiantly charges into an interaction in an attempt to save a woman from enjoying herself, while she is in a provocative conversation with another man.

It normally begins with the "nice guy" witnessing another man successfully flirting with a woman in a fashion which he personally believes is unbefitting to her. He then chooses to ignore the fact that the woman is actually enjoying herself, and if she wanted to end the interaction and leave, there is nothing preventing her from doing so. Unlike the woman, perhaps the "nice guy" cannot distinguish the difference between the confident man's words and their intent. In order to protect the idealized image that he as of this woman, along with his own personal worldview, the "nice guy" feels that he must quickly act before any further contradictory evidence presents itself.

However, for this man to even feel the right to intrude on the interaction, he must first believe that he is more entitled to the woman than the other man. Thus the "nice guy's" entire actions are derived from an unhealthy view with regards to entitlement. Ironically, he is also using this unhealthy sense of entitlement to justify that he himself is good enough for the woman. He believes that if the woman is willing to receive the "cocky guy," then she would also be likely to entertain him. He thinks: "I am not only richer and slightly better looking than 'Mr. Cocky' over there, but most importantly of all, I am a nice guy!"

However, as we know, a "nice guy's" actions are often extremely dishonest. Firstly, it is terribly condescending to treat a woman as if she does not have the ability to choose the people with whom she interacts. After injecting himself into the interaction, the "nice guy" then proceeds to lie to the woman about his actual intentions. His desire is not to actually provide for the welfare of the woman, but instead to either protect his own worldview, win the woman over for himself, or at the very least feel validation for delivering some self-contrived social justice.

When a man who does not fit society's pre-conscribed ideal is seen with an extraordinarily beautiful woman, jealous onlookers grasp for any explanation which will protect their worldviews. People often vehemently reject anything that goes against their personal long withstanding world models. They say that the man must be rich or used manipulative pick-up artist techniques to get her. They do not want to believe that the man was able to improve himself to a level that the woman found him attractive. Men may attack this man, since they rather believe their inability to attract woman is due to circumstances that they have no control over, and want to keep playing role of the poor victim. Even some women may attack and shame this man because he challenges the world model which they rely on to know which men they should value.

One night during my time at university, I was out at a bar with my friend Jeff. As previously mentioned in a past anecdote, Jeff was a bit of a player and a natural with women. The group of women that Jeff and I were currently speaking with contained a mutual acquaintance who knew me via another engineering friend group. She was somewhat perplexed why Jeff and I were hanging out together. She told me: "You are such as nice guy, and Jeff is an asshole. Why are the two of you together? You are nothing like Jeff." What she was really saying was that I was not the type of guy who deserved the same attention that Jeff was getting, and seeing us together was conflicting with her personal world model. That night her friend proceeded to go home with Jeff.

When people meet you for the first time, their minds quickly go to work trying to sort you into a specific box. This is why women are intrigued by a man that is a bit mysterious. Their minds will intently focus on the man until they feel that they have successfully categorized him. This is also why it is imperative to establish a man to woman frame (i.e. express your honest interest for a woman) as soon as possible. Once a woman has categorized you as being unsex worthy (put you in the friend zone), it will be increasingly difficult to get yourself re-categorized. A woman does not want to risk jeopardizing her current world model by calling her past judgments into question.

Self-improvement can often disrupt the realities of those around you. Lifelong friends may try to hold you back because they may interpret your success as a threat to their own world models. If someone with a similar background and history as them suddenly becomes successful in an area of their life, then they have to reflect back on their own status. To protect their own world models, people may even convince themselves that you were always naturally a certain way from the start and choose to dismiss your transformation.

By fitting a certain image, you attain social proof on the societal level. If you can perfectly fit society's publicized narrative of a high quality man for a woman, then feel free to play the game by the official written rules. However, if you do not perfectly fit society's image, then perhaps you should not be spending all your time and resources trying to force yourself into a mold in which you cannot comfortably fit. Even many of the men who do nicely fit this mold, and who I believe should be crushing it in life, are still hitting way below their potential because they are operating with a constrained view of the world.

You are not going to be able to reprogram your local culture so that all women find value in what you personally believe to be your better qualities. Many women would find more value in the fact that you are friends with Justin Bieber, than the fact that you are the CEO of your own company. This is why the second half of this book will focus on the internal qualities and behaviors which women unanimously find attractive and which are primarily independent of your external happenstances.

This leads us to frame control. Your frame is the outer projection of your inner beliefs. A person with a strong frame has a fixed sense of reality which draws in other people. A person with a weak frame allows their beliefs and actions to be molded by the will of others. Women are attracted to a man who has a strong sense of certainty about his beliefs and values. A woman will often challenge you in order to check if your frame holds strong or if it will falter and bend to her will. A woman thinks that if you cannot handle her alone, what chance do you have against the rest of the world?

Most women's frames are formed via a combination of how they personally view themselves and the social narrative that they are taught from a young age. Thus if you find yourself operating within the frame of a woman who has bought into the standard social narrative, be ready for this woman to have the standard expectations that go along with it. These expectations can include paying for her dinners, taking her out to certain events, buying her an expensive engagement ring or house, in addition to any other actions whose sole purpose is to prove that you are deserving of her.

Do not misinterpret this and think that you should not be a giving, providing and loving person. If your actions truly come from an altruistic place, then there is nothing wrong with your generosity. The problem is that many men are fully convinced they are acting unselfishly, while in reality they want something in return. These men have bought into the false social contract that through performing certain actions or simply just being a "good guy," that in return they deserve to be rewarded with affections, admiration or sex.

If you are in a relationship and operating within this provider frame, then be prepared to be lambasted when you do not meet some nonsensical expectation. This anger is often directed not at your immediate actions but at an underlying cause. While some women are by nature very materialistic and status obsessed, many other women just view these gifts, favors or expectations as external consolation prizes to compensate for their man not being himself of high enough value. They desire something flashy to show off to their girlfriends, because they cannot show off their actual man. Just like their men, these women choose to double down on the false social narrative that having a domesticated man who provides them with everything that they want will make them happy.

Both men and women together are being deceived by the same false paradigm. Men are confused by why, that even after continually sacrificing themselves to provide for their women, their women only seem more upset and less interested in them. On the flip side, women are confused by why they are still unsatisfied even after their men do and provide them with everything that they ask for. The reason for these misunderstandings is that women want to be with a man with a strong frame, which in turn makes them feel secure. If a man lacks boundaries, and can be easily manipulated or controlled by a woman to get what she wants, a woman feels emotionally betrayed.

If your number one concern is pleasing a woman, then by always putting yourself second, you are showing how little you care for yourself. If you do not believe that you are worth much, why should a woman think anything different? By constantly sacrificing yourself in an attempt to please a woman, you are not earning her love but instead losing her respect. Again, this does not mean that you should neither compromise with nor provide for your woman. What is meant is that you should act because you want to, not because you feel obligated, socially pressured, or want something in return.

Women will often relent on pettier desires when offered the opportunity to be with a man with a strong frame. When a man with a strong frame provides a woman with a gift, the woman will fully appreciate it. She will know that the gift comes from a place of benevolence, rather than it just being an installment payment towards her love and approval.

Having a strong frame allows you to create a reality into which you can bring other people. When you are so incredibly sure of yourself and your actions, others may even start to question their own long held beliefs. During a moment of uncertainty within an interaction, the person which holds the stronger frame will always prevail. The person with the weaker frame will often then choose to buy into the reality of the person holding the stronger frame. This principle can hold true regardless of the validity of one's beliefs, a result which unfortunately lets charismatic leaders dupe their followers.

If you believe that what you have to say has value and you do not appear concerned by what others think of you, then others will more often buy into your frame and listen to what you have to say. Likewise, if you approach a girl with the belief that she will enjoy talking to you, then she will more likely feel the same. When every one of your actions is executed with absolute confidence and authority, very few people will question if what you did was correct. When you act timidly and are looking to others for approval, in addition to appearing weak and unattractive, your actions will more often be called into question.

By having a strong sense of self which you unapologetically project, you can bring people into your reality and set the terms of an interaction. Instead of worrying if you are good enough for a woman, you can tell a woman what is of value to you, and have her measure herself up against your standards. Women will be more attracted to you when they know that you have standards, and feel that they have impressed you enough to meet them. With regards to relationships, it is important to frame the type of relationship you want from the beginning so that expectations will be met. Women will often agree to boundaries and expectations if they are established early on through honest communication.

Furthermore, with a strong frame you can even project your expectations onto another person. People want to remain congruent to their own self-image, and even more often to the views that others hold of them. After being brought into your frame and view of reality, you can project an identity onto a person that they will want to live up to. When you show that in your reality that a certain behavior is either acceptable or unacceptable, the other person will likely follow suit.

Thus if you frame leaving the library to go on an instant coffee date with you as being normal, then the woman you just met will more likely comply. Likewise, a woman is more likely to go home with you after a party if you are holding a strong nonjudgmental and outcome independent frame. This principle should be used passively to show confidence and self-assurance rather than for the active manipulation of others.

If you have a strong frame and believe that being either short or bald should have no influence on your desirability to woman, then many women will hold these said features less against you. It's often your own insecurity which you project onto women that they find unattractive, not so much the thing that actually causes it. Moreover, the things which you cannot fix about yourself you can choose to feature. When you accept a flaw and remain confident despite it, more attraction can be generated than if you lacked the so called flaw altogether. As with acquiring an abundance mentality, establishing a strong personal frame takes time and effort. You must first come to know yourself, what you value and your personal boundaries.

When placed in unfamiliar situations, people observe and mirror the emotions of those around them. If you are holding a strong frame, then others will subconsciously mirror your reactions. If you feel that there is nothing awkward about striking up a conversation with an unknown woman, the woman will likely mirror the emotions that you are showing.

If you are calm, friendly and honest, then the probability of a good response is high. However, if you feel awkward and nervous, a woman's emotional state will feed off your behavioral cues and she will feel the same. The next chapter speaks specifically on how women experience emotion.

Chapter 6: Emotional Domain vs. Logical Domain

"Attraction is generated not by what you logically say, but by what you emotionally convey."

Engineers and other technically minded people spend the majority of their time performing in the logical domain. This is because we know that how we feel about a problem is not going to actually solve it. However, if your problem is attracting women, then you must learn to operate in the emotional domain. People don't remember so much what you said or did, but rather how you made them feel. Memory is closely linked to emotions. People often make decisions based on their emotions, and then subsequently backwards rationalize to decide on the reasons why they made them.

A huge error that many men make when trying to attract women is attempting to logically convince a woman that she should find them attractive. A man will often brag about his accomplishments and material possessions in an attempt to impress a woman. The majority of women will find such behavior crass, and believe that the man is overcompensating for something else. I used to try to impress woman by mentioning my prestigious university degree along with the fact that I had a small student-built satellite in space. Given that my underlying intention from the start was to try to impress, this often did not yield good results.

It's much better that a woman finds out about your accomplishments organically, rather than through you listing them off right away in your initial conversation. It is good to show traits such as having a good career and social status, since they let a woman rationalize her attraction for you based on societal constructs. However, a woman's initial attraction towards you will not be primarily based on such things, but instead on almost solely how you make her feel.

While everyone spends part of their time operating in both the emotional and logical domains, women spend more time communicating their emotions, while men communicate information. Men bond by coming together to solve common problems. When a man encounters a problem, his mind automatically starts to search for a solution. When one man consults another man regarding a particular issue, the inquiring man appreciates a clear and logical response. When a woman consults a man on an issue, she is often more interested in having her feelings understood than receiving an actual solution. A man thinks that he is helping the woman when he quickly proposes solutions to her problem, while the woman interprets this behavior as the man not taking the time to understand how she truly feels.

Next time you are in a room with people, listen to the conversations between members in all male and female groups. In the male groups you will hear logical advice and concrete points. For example: "You should mark the support beams before installing the dry wall."; "The newer engine model provides much more power than the last."; "You may want to diversify your investment portfolio to include more bonds." and "That was the completely wrong play for the quarterback to run." Discussions within all female groups will contain more emotionally based conversation. For example: "Amber knows that I *hate* working on Tuesdays, but she purposely keeps scheduling my shifts on them."; "I *feel very overwhelmed* right now since my in-laws are over."; "I am a bit *nervous* for my date on Saturday." and "Do you think he *likes* me?"

The next time a woman comes to you with a problem, rather than instantaneously providing her with potential solutions, instead engage her emotional side. Ask her how a situation makes her feel, empathize with her, and validate that she is correct for feeling the way she does. However, these actions should come from a place where you are honestly trying to understand her emotions, and not just trying to win points by telling her what you think she wants to hear.

To show that you have listened and understand her, repeat back to the woman what she has told you. Most women already know from the start what they should do to solve a problem and just want their emotions to be understood. Women get feelings off their chest by sharing the feelings with others. In many ways, this actually lets you off the hook. You are often not required to actually solve the woman's problem at all, but only empathize with her for having it. Likewise, when debating or arguing with a woman, it is often better to try to change her mood and not her mind.

Women love to feel a range of emotions, which is a reason why drama and romance books are the top selling categories in the United States. The human brain pays more attention to contrast and changes than it does to things that remain constant. This makes sense evolutionarily, since changes in one's normal environment can prelude potential danger. This is why we quickly notice new smells and sounds while typical conditions tend fade into the background. Thus while the average emotions in a conversation should remain positive, negative dips keep a conversation more interesting and lively for a woman. The negative dips don't need to be an insult or backhanded compliment. They actually often occur naturally when you are unafraid to offer honest opinions, do not filter your speech and are not actively trying to please someone.

For an emotion to even be classified as positive, it needs to be referenced against some other baseline emotion. I refer to this concept as the woman's response to the 1st derivative of her emotions. The brain more clearly registers changes in emotions than its constant emotional state. This is why people can slowly fall into depression without immediately recognizing it. If you bring positive emotions to a woman, she will take notice of this positive change in her emotional state and attribute it to you. A change from a negative to a positive emotion is much more powerful than only providing positive emotions, since the mind more clearly registers it. Thus if an interaction initially starts poorly, the more powerful the effect of turning it around will be.

In our society, there is a growing addiction to emotional stimulus. Within moments of waking up, we are already checking our smartphones. Every few seconds you can give the gift of validation by "liking" a new post in your Facebook feed. The media broadcasts nonstop "breaking news" to spike your emotions by either trying to terrify or outrage you. A club DJ cannot even make it through a full three minute song, before he needs to start a new track to provide novelty and get people jumping up and down. In places like nightclubs, people want to overload their senses and bask in the emotions they are experiencing in an attempt to completely drown out their logical minds. Recognizing this stimulation addiction makes it even more important to understand why purely logical conversations — lacking emotional undertones — will completely fall flat with many women.

The first step to naturally dramatizing a conversation is by honestly expressing yourself and not needing approval for every word you speak. Additionally, you can work on speaking more descriptively and expressing emotion. A good story teller paints pictures in the listener's minds and makes them feel the emotions of those in their story.

The majority of attraction in a conversation is generated *not by what you logically say, but by what you emotionally convey*. It is not *what* you say that matters, but *how and why* you say it. The *how* referencing the emotions being sub-communicated and the *why* being the intent behind them. A major breakthrough for me was when I discovered the huge difference between conveying emotions and conveying information while in a conversation. When it comes to building attraction, the subject matter of a conversation is often almost trivial. It's the emotions that are sub-communicated that are of actual importance.

I remember spending one evening talking to a girl and telling her all about myself. While she learned a great deal of factual information about me, her emotional side was left completely unengaged. The next weekend I met a girl and started an entertaining make-believe conversation with her about forming an *Oceans 11* like team and then going to Paris to steal the Mona Lisa. She spent that evening as my accomplice crafting a fictitious plot to rob the Louvre.

At the end of this evening, I got her number and we ended up dating for a short time after that. Upon meeting on our first date, I realized that that she literally did not know anything about me. I had not told her my age, profession, interests, etc. Nothing personal at all! She had made the decision to meet with me based solely off the positive and fun emotions that she had experienced the night we met.

Another evening, I remember having a similar make-believe conversation with a different girl, about how we were going to move to Dublin together and live above a bakery so that she should could pursue her dream to be a professional violin player. When her friend came back from the bathroom, this girl started excitedly jumping up and down and screaming to her that we were going to move to Dublin. Her friend, who was not invited into our fantasy world, understandably had a puzzled look on her face.

Although based off of completely factitious scenarios, the emotions that these women experienced in our imaginative adventures together were real. A connection was built between us as if we had actually gone through these experiences together. They felt emotions towards me in the same way that you feel emotions towards a character in a book or movie. These women had no logical reasons to like me, other than the fact that I was enjoyable to be with. They did not know anything factual about me, nor had I directly demonstrated something in front of them that would have warranted admiration. However, my behavior did communicate that I was a self-fulfilled person who was not seeking value from them, but willing to provide it.

I noticed that in conversations with women which would go nowhere, that I was conveying only information and barely any emotions. Instead of asking the question: "Why doesn't she like me?" I started asking the question: "Why should she like me?" Most men make the mistake of trying to answers this question using logical reasons: wealth, career, status, looks, etc. Instead, I recommend reflecting on your conversations to see if you provided the woman with any emotional reasons to connect with you. Remember, decisions are often made based on emotions and then rationalized later using logic. Having logical reasons to find you attractive will benefit you much more after a subconscious emotional connection has first been established.

Through subconscious body language we broadcast our current emotional state. You can often tell a person's emotional state just by looking at them. A person who is positive and loving life radiates positive vibrations. People want to be around a happy and fun person because that person's energy is contagious. Likewise, people want to avoid a person whose low energy and negativity they feel will bring them down. The law of state transference declares that your current emotions will be broadcast and felt by those around you. This is even further amplified when you hold a strong frame and are commanding an interaction.

When you approach a woman while feeling nervous or awkward, the woman will likely feel these same feelings inside herself. Your feelings about the situation instantaneously become her own. If you feel that you are beneath her, you will never get beneath her. Firstly, life will rarely give you more than you ask for. Secondly, a woman will sense that you are unsure of yourself and thus automatically be skeptical about you. Even worse is when you try to act cool while clearly being nervous and thus appear to the woman as incongruent. Only through practice, can you squelch the underlying fear which is blocking the transmission of any honest positive intentions and emotions.

Once you master your own emotions, and learn to draw your emotional state from within yourself instead of from external influences, you will have an incredible power over those around you. If you are able to hold a strong positive frame, even in the face of another person's negativity, that person will often be forced to adapt your frame. Thus a girl, who may initially be rude or ignore you, will likely be intrigued to why her dismissal did not affect your emotional state. She may then question her own negativity — feel out of place — and start to warm up to you.

When you broadcast that you are self-fulfilled, women will be incredibly drawn to you. A person who is self-fulfilled does not seek value from others, and thus is more likely to provide it. Women will want to absorb these emotions from you which will allow them to let loose and forget about their own insecurities. Broadcasting a fun and nonjudgmental vibe will allow the woman you are with to experience the same enjoyment and freedom from judgment. While in a social gatherings, positive emotions and freedom from judgment are generally what people desire the most. Feeling free from judgment will allow a woman to honestly express herself to you. This shared openness and vulnerability will then enable an emotional connection to develop.

Developing emotional intelligence is critical to becoming successful with women. Some people have an incredibly difficult time reading the emotional state of others. The first step is to concentrate on being aware of how you are making others feel. Periodically throughout social interactions, ask yourself the question: "How am I making this person feel?" When you sense that you may have made someone uncomfortable through your words or actions, apologize for it. Showing empathy will help rectify the situation and put the woman at ease by demonstrating social awareness. Women feel comfortable being around men who can read their emotions and do not pressure them into uncomfortable situations.

Calibration is the ability to adjust your actions so that you act within the presumed standards of your current company or environment. Location, culture, and time of day all make a difference when it comes to what is deemed appropriate. Even if done with a super strong frame, dancing on top of your desk during lunch hour would likely come off as inappropriate. However, if done at the company Christmas party, the entire office may join in. Likewise, the accepted behavior at 9 PM at a bar when everyone is just arriving is different than at 2 AM. Knowing how to quickly adapt to an environment is a skill that requires social awareness. Analyze how others are behaving in your environment to ensure that your actions are within bounds.

Being able to evaluate a person on the emotional spectrum will give you incredible insight into their behavior. So often people seem to act irrationally and we wonder why they choose to make the decisions that they do. However, if we take a look at their actions in the emotional domain, then the reasons behind their choices often become clear.

Emotional decisions can fly in the face of logic. You can logically provide a woman with what she desires while simultaneously betraying her emotions. Women often like to test a man's resolve, especially when it appears to be weakening. While one might initially imagine that a woman would be made happy by getting what she wants, on a deeper level she will feel disappointed if it was due to you sacrificing your own personal convictions.

While her logical mind may be satisfied, emotionally she may become disappointed or unsettled. By pushing through a personal boundary that you had previously established, she may now respect you less as a man and worry that you will be susceptible to manipulation from others. This will incite doubt about your fortitude and lead her to feeling insecure, which for a woman translates to feeling unloved and uncared for.

On the flip side, when a woman feels that you are too good for her, she may try to sabotage your success. She does this out of a fear that if you improve yourself to much that you might end up leaving her. While feeding her boyfriend fattening food and asking him to skip going to the gym does not make logical sense, emotionally it gives the women a greater sense of security. Women with scarcity mentalities of their own will be willing to trade your success and growth for their own security. This statement is made assuming that all other things are equal and you are not asking the woman to somehow sacrifice her own career, personal life or other responsibilities for you. You must reassure a woman that you plan to grow together, and you will bring her up with you and not leave her behind.

My friend Fred once promised his girlfriend that he would help her study for an exam that she was nervous about passing. The exam was on marketing, but contained a fair amount of applied mathematics. Since my friend studied engineering, his girlfriend was confident that he would be able to assist her with the math. While my friend could indeed solve the equations, having not taken the course himself, he did not know when it was appropriate to apply each formula. Thus without first studying the material himself, he could not teach it to his girlfriend.

Although he tried his best to do so, there was physically not enough time for my friend to teach himself an entire course of material and then reteach it to his girlfriend before her exam. She ended up failing her exam, and being incredibly upset with my friend. Although logically it does not make sense for her to blame Fred for trying his best to help her, emotionally she still felt betrayed. She had trusted that my friend would be able to adequately prepare her to pass the exam, and in failing to do so, he had betrayed her confidence in him.

Responses in the emotional domain are based on current inputs which are often independent from past events. You may have a perfect track record, but a single slip-up could result in a violent outcry. For many women, the present moment is more important than your track record. If you make a promise to a woman that you fail to live up to — even for reasons which are entirely beyond your control — she may still be upset. Even when logically there is no reason to blame you, emotionally she may still feel betrayed. She has trusted you to take care of something, and you have failed. On some level, this failure makes her question the trust she has that you will take care of her. This feeling of loss of security can then lead to her acting out in an attempt to either validate or repudiate her fears.

This fear will trigger in her memory all the previous times that you have let her down. In these situations, it is important to never enter a logical argument. What the woman wants is instantaneous proof that you love and care for her, and this can only be conveyed via the emotional domain. You need to show compassion in the present moment, not bring up all the other things that you do for her in an attempt to logically convince her that you care. Logical conversation can take place after the emotional response has settled.

When it comes to generating attraction, trying to engage a woman logically will most likely yield failure from the start. Not only will you be more likely to bore her, but you will have to contend with the personal, family and cultural constructs which have been imbedded into her since birth. All the core principles of attraction are directly accessed via the emotional domain. The only people with whom logically trying to barter for a relationship or sex will work are prostitutes, people deep in scarcity and those forced into compromise. A person must emotionally feel attraction, not be reasoned logically into feeling it.

However, after attraction is established, you may still initially need to provide a woman with a logical justification that allows her to act on it. Societal double standards have conditioned women to feel extremely shameful about ever appearing like a slut. This is why you must be discreet with a woman while in public. A woman may want to give you her phone number, but refuse to do so if her friends are watching. She may not want her friends to judge her for giving a random man her number after only fifteen minutes of conversation. This same principle of discretion also applies to public kissing and other physical contact.

While external judgment is often a factor with which you must contend, so is internal judgment. Unless the woman is highly self-assured, she may also want to protect the self-image that she has of herself. When her logical mind finally catches up with her emotions, a woman is faced with making the conscious choice to be with a man. After a woman mentally acknowledges what she is feeling, a fear of judgment may prevent her from acting on it. Having a token excuse such as inviting you up for "coffee" or over to watch "Netflix and chill," lets a woman absolve herself from the shame that society places on women who deliberately initiate intimacy. Instead of having to contend with the fact that she directly asked you to spend the night, she can rationalize the experience along the lines of the more socially accepted narrative that things just naturally and spontaneously took their course.

While you should never lie, you should be aware that some women will want you to provide them with an excuse with which they can use to justify their actions. Since the only purpose of this excuse is to appease a woman's rational mind, what the actual excuse is often does not matter. Thus it could potentially be as outlandish as inviting her to come over to play Mario Kart at 2 AM.

The act of thinking too much and over analyzing a situation will bring you out of the emotional domain and into the logical domain. When you are stuck in your head, you are failing to be completely present to the current moment, and thus cannot broadcast fully honest emotions. You are not present if you are filtering your thoughts out of fear of them being inadequate, constantly thinking ahead about future conversation topics, or not able to let go of a past mistake.

These types of behaviors reveal that you are putting pressure on yourself. This emotional unease is then transferred onto the woman. By being completely in the present moment, you free yourself from past pain and any future fears. Being present provides one with an authentic demeanor which is detected by women, and lets them know that the emotions you are communicating are legitimate. You cannot have a hidden future objective if your actions are derived completely from the present moment. After a woman trusts that you are communicating honestly to her, attraction can be generated by displaying the traits and behaviors described in the following chapters of this book.

Chapter 7: The Four C's of Female Attraction

"Cleanliness, Confidence, Congruence, Consistency"

Before discussing the specific behaviors of an attractive man, we must first lay the underlying foundation upon which all attraction is built. Cleanliness, confidence, congruence and consistency are the four core traits that women initially check for in a man. A man who lacks these traits will have problems generating even slight amounts of attraction. However, a man who embodies all these traits will have women naturally drawn to him.

1. Cleanliness

Cleanliness is the easiest trait to master. When it comes to approaching total strangers, the first thing that you will be judged on is your appearance. Fortunately for men, women put much less importance on a man's physical appearance then men do on the physical appearances of women. However, a woman will be conscious of the amount of effort a man makes to properly care for himself. How much a man cares for his appearance often mirrors how he views himself. It only takes a small bit of effort to look your best. In comparison, women often spend hours working on their appearance before heading out for an evening.

For beginners, cleanliness has a heightened importance. Since you will still be actively building an attractive personality, you will be more dependent on your physical appearance. Men who already have superior skills in meeting woman can often greatly slack with their hygiene and still be surprisingly successful. However, if this is not yet you, then there is no reason to handicap yourself from the start. It's easier to act the part of an attractive man if you look the part.

After polling multiple women, the following general consensus was formed regarding the physical details of a man to which women pay the most attention. Women pay attention to these following areas of a man's appearance, because it is what they pay attention to on themselves and other women. It takes only minimal effort for you to address these areas. Apart from these specific areas, the obvious additions of being in good shape and living a healthier lifestyle will of course be to your advantage.

Shoes: With so many women being obsessed with their own shoes, why would you think that they would not care about yours? Wearing a pair of more stylish non-sport dress shoes is better than wearing a pair of old sneakers. If you are in a nice nightclub, the bouncer at the door probably already screened you based on your shoes.

Clean Finger Nails: Women are the usual clients at nail salons, where they may spend exorbitant amounts of money on an area of their body which men will likely not even notice. (Hint: Complimenting a woman on her nails can score you some points, since it is unlikely that many other men have ever done so.) While there is no need to get a manicure, you should keep your own nails trimmed and clean.

Clean Teeth and Mouth: Brush your teeth, use whitening products, and use mouthwash to prevent bad breath.

Remove Excess Facial Hair: Remove the hair on the back of your neck, the front of your neck, in your nose, ears and between your eyebrows.

Wear Well-Fitting Clothes: Make sure your clothing fits properly. The staff at most stores are willing to take your measurements to help ensure that you are buying the correct sizes. For non-formal settings, there is no need to overdress. It is usually enough to just look neat and clean. Look at how other men who are successful with women dress and base your outfits off their styles.

2. Confidence

A confident man does not need a woman to like him to feel good about himself. His beliefs about himself and his self-worth are not dependent on the approval of others. He says what he truly believes, and not just what he thinks others want to hear. He is unapologetic about who he is and what he desires. This confidence is derived from the fact that the man fully accepts himself, including all his imperfections.

Closely related to the concept of entitlement, confidence can also come in situational form. For many men, approaching and meeting attractive women is something that is far outside their realm of comfort. Thus the confidence they have in other areas of their lives does not translate to meeting women. In contrast, a person with core confidence has a deep trust in their faculties which permeates into all situations both known and new.

On multiple occasions, I have started a conversation with an attractive woman at a nightlife venue, only to learn that it was her one night off of the week and she had chosen to spend it sitting alone at the same bar where she normally serves drinks. These beautiful women's confidence and sense of entitlement are so limited to a specific environment that they choose to spend their limited free time at the same place where they work. I have watched the confidence of these women drop the instant they step out the door of a nightclub and exit its bubble of constant validation.

A generic lack of confidence can stem from the deep-seeded insecurity that you are unworthy of the approval or love of others. Shame is one of the most dreadful of human emotions. Some people have lived unfortunate lives where they have been conditioned into feeling shame for simply existing. This is the most toxic form of shame, where you feel that you are not worth much as person and believe that your personal desires could only ever be a burden to others.

To avoid being chastised, such individuals work tirelessly at meeting the expectations that others have of them. They believe that the only way to ward off pain and gain approval is by pleasing everyone but themselves. They never even pause and ask themselves what it is that they truly want. If you can relate to this, then you will need to reevaluate your self-worth in general and come to the realization that you are as deserving of love as everyone else.

Building self-confidence will take more effort than simply buying a new pair of shoes. Confidence results from being able to draw from past experiences. There is no way to gain experience other than by putting in the necessary work and placing yourself outside of your comfort zone. While literature can provide you with the knowledge that you need to be successful, it will never take the place of actual experience. You could read a hundred books on skiing prior to taking on the slopes, but you will still likely fall the first few times out. You should not view these falls as failures. Your actual goal is to learn how to ski, and with respect to that endeavor you are succeeding. Learning from your mistakes is what is most important. The people who improve the fastest are the ones that are not afraid to fail early and fail often.

Since confidence comes from experience, you may be wondering: "What's a guy to do who completely lacks any past experiences?" This is where the old phrase "fake it till you make it" holds some truth. While I don't recommend "faking it," since it breaks our rules about honesty and can make you appear incongruent, it is still catchier than the more accurate phrase: "Accept your current limitations, but do not let them prevent you from putting yourself in new situations which may allow you to acquire through experience the skills required to be successful." People who are so called "faking it" are still placing themselves in unfamiliar situations and forcing themselves to either sink or swim. Their ability to survive these situations, regardless of their success, is what grows their core confidence.

3. Congruence

A woman will look for congruence in your thoughts, words and actions. Given that the majority of communication is non-verbal, there is no such thing as a perfect "pick-up line." A woman will look to see if what you say matches how you say it. Does the tone and cadence of your voice match that of a person who is confident? Are you frantically searching in the back of your head for something to say, or are your completely present to the moment? Does your posture match that of an open person, or someone who is insecure? Is your face showing emotions that you are pretending not to have? Are you clearly smitten by her, but still trying to act casual by nervously discussing the weather?

When your thoughts, words, and actions are not aligned, a woman will feel that there is something off about you or that you are to some extent lying to her. She may think that you are putting on a false act and not acting true to who you really are, and she is likely right. Even though you act indifferent to having her validation, you may still be showing indications that say otherwise. Instead of speaking freely to her like you would to your friends, you may instead be filtering your words and actively trying to make her like you. When you are stuck in your head and out of the present moment, you are showing that you are not at ease and do not feel in full control of the interaction.

Here is an extremely common example of how incongruence appears within an initial interaction between a man and a woman. A man approaches a woman at a bar. Given the environment, this action alone automatically tells the woman that the man is interested in her. However, the man starts the conversation by saying: "Do you know what time the bar closes?" Already this is an immediate act of incongruence by the man. The context and action of the man approaching the woman says: "I want to get to know you." While his literal words say: "I am primarily here because I desire information about the bar's hours of operation." The woman knows why the man really approached her. By pretending that the reason was to ask for the closing time, he has lied to her within their first seconds of meeting. If the woman was actually interested in meeting someone, she is now likely disappointed that the man who approached her lacks the confidence to show his true intentions.

As their conversation continues, the man then asks what the woman does for work and pretends to be interested in it. The man is primarily thinking in his head: "I hope this woman keeps talking to me." But the words from the man's mouth are communicating an insincere interest in the woman's work as a nutritionist. On top of this, due to being nervous, the arm with which the man is holding his drink is slightly shaking. All of this tells the woman that the man is trying to hide his true intent and emotions. Eventually, the incongruence between the man's thoughts, words and actions causes the woman to become uncomfortable and excuse herself from the conversation.

If you are nervous to the point of stuttering and shaking while talking to a woman, it is better for you tell the woman that you are a bit nervous than to ignore the effect that your behavior is having on her. By verbally acknowledging your nervousness, it will help remove any awkwardness in the interaction. While you may not get points for confidence, you will at least receive some for honesty.

There is some validity to the phrase "just be yourself." You should avoid becoming incongruent as a result of pretending to be someone that you are not. Incongruence shows women that you are not a truly confident and self-secure person and thus kills attraction. Women will ignore all signals from you if they believe that they are not honest signals. However, if these honest signals are still portraying you as an unattractive man, then of course "just being yourself" is not going to work. You must work to become the best version of yourself. This is done not by changing your interests or passions, but by cultivating a core confidence which will let you freely express your true self via attractive behaviors.

When you are acting congruently, but behaving in a nervous or unattractive manner, then women will label you as that "nice shy guy" and see your "hidden" interest in them as being "cute." When you are acting incongruently, and thus by definition in an unattractive manner, then women will label you as being "creepy," "a try-hard," or "weird." It is only when you are acting congruently in an attractive manner that women will find you attractive. These specific behaviors of an attractive man will be discussed later in detail. It's important to first understand the concepts of congruence and consistency, since for any behavior to be found attractive it must be presented in these ways.

4. Consistency

Women will want to verify that you actually are who you appear to be. Males of every species often use deception as a tactic to attract women. Women want a man to remain consistent over time and in all situations. Being consistent allows for a woman to build comfort and trust with you. Women use "congruence tests" to try to throw you off balance and break what they might think is a false composure. These tests are used to illicit a response from you which is not consistent with how they perceive you to be thus far. If a woman detects a change, she will believe that on some level that she has previously been lied to, and thus may feel disappointed, angry, and/or disgusted.

A woman often uses congruence tests (consciously and unconsciously) when trying to categorize a new man in her life (short-term consistency) or re-evaluate a man who she feels has shown weakness or changed (long-term consistency). You won't get these tests often in environments where a woman already knows you well and has long ago categorized you. However, in first encounters, especially ones where you are interested in courting a woman, congruence tests are extremely common and often a form of flirting.

You should not fear or become aggravated when a woman tests you in an initial interaction. Being tested is a sign that a woman has some interest in you. If she was not interested in you at all, she would simply just dismiss you or make polite conversation. Instead, she is trying to verify in an accelerated manner that the person she just met is the cool, confident and congruent person that he appears to be. To pass these tests, you only need to recognize that you are being tested and not have it affect your demeanor. Your best action may even be to ignore her remarks or questions altogether. You should not feel the need to prove or qualify yourself to a woman that you just met. Later on, when you have developed greater self-confidence and abundance, you will become unresponsive to congruence tests as a result of literally just not caring.

Here are common congruence tests that women give along with some potential answers.

Common Congruence Tests

Test: The woman stares into your eyes to see if you can comfortably hold eye contact.
Answer: Comfortably hold eye contact.

Test: She brings up a sexual topic and looks to see if it makes you uncomfortable.
Answer: Speak about the topic with confidence and do not immediately shy away from it.

Test: Compares you to another man saying: "I think the waiter is cute."

Answer: Do not appear jealous, and perhaps even agree with her.

Test: Introduces you to her guy friend who is physically superior to you.

Answer: Do not appear intimidated, and joke with him about the girl. "How can you be in public with this girl. Haha."

Test: Points out one of your short comings.

Answer: Do not become defensive. Re-frame it as a strength or laugh about it. Show that you fully embrace all of who you are and that her opinion does not concern you.

Consistency also comes into play in long-term relationships. In these cases, consistency is tested by reevaluating a man's personal boundaries. A man must set personal boundaries in his life and not let them be compromised by others, himself or his partner. A woman wants to be with a man that she respects, and if the man does not respect himself, why should she? If a woman knows that she can manipulate her man, she will then worry how her man will stand against the rest of the world. This will result in the woman feeling insecure and uncared for. This insecurity can then take the form of anger, resentment or infidelity.

Some men wonder why that when they finally relent and do what their woman wants, it only makes her angrier or more emotional. This is because while you are logically providing her with what she has asked for, emotionally you are betraying her by showing a lack of conviction. You must be unafraid to call out a woman's behavior when she crosses one of your boundaries. While this may cause tension in the short-term, the long-lasting sense of strength and security it provides to the woman will only strengthen the relationship.

Chapter 8: Generating Attraction

"As to methods, there may be a million and then some, but principles are few. The man who grasps principles can successfully select his own methods. The man who tries methods, ignoring principles, is sure to have trouble."
-Ralph Waldo Emerson

While most people want instant gratification and quick fixes to their problems, there is no magic pill that will instantaneously make you successful with women. However, I am still going to try to indulge you by providing eight rules that when followed will dramatically increase your success. You can begin adapting the following behaviors, even if you do not yet have a full understanding or internalization of the deeper principles at play.

While the long term goal is to develop into a man who naturally embodies these attractive qualities, through conscious awareness you can still use the following rules to immediately start fixing some of your most egregious errors. Reflect back on your interactions with women, and try to identify the times that you made any of the following common mistakes outlined in this chapter.

When it comes to one's success, it is often not what you do, but rather what you specifically do not do which makes the difference. Simply ceasing certain unattractive behavioral patterns will set you apart from the vast majority of men and allow you to instantly generate attraction in women. I would recommend focusing on only one habit at a time. Otherwise, you may become self-conscious to a point where constant self-reflection will keep you trapped in your head.

1. Hold Strong Eye Contact and Smile

Being able to hold strong eye contact is extremely important. Women often first judge a man based on his ability to hold eye contact. Strong yet comfortable unwavering eye contact is an incredibly hard signal to fake that shows confidence, along with a fact that you have nothing to hide. In addition to eye contact, simply smiling will make you appear as a friendlier, happier and more relaxed person to be around. Without a slight smile on your face, strong eye contact can come off as intimidating and aggressive. Additionally, when approaching a woman, you should at least appear to be in a relaxed state, and not be tensing up in expectation of a potentially negative response.

2. Do not Barter for Attention or Affection

Do not buy drinks, give insincere compliments, or perform actions whose sole purpose is to make a woman like you. Doing any of these things is the equivalent of trying to buy a woman's affection. It also creates a feeling of indebtedness. No one wants to feel indebted, especially to someone that they don't know. While the transaction of material possessions is clearly apparent, we often barter on a more subtle level through the giving of verbal compliments and affirmations.

Do not simply tell a girl what you think she wants to hear. Firstly, she knows when you are doing so. And secondly, she will respect you more for having your own opinions. There is nothing wrong with disagreeing on a subject. A woman will enjoy speaking to someone who challenges her, and is not simply agreeing with her in an attempt to win her over. Let there be some natural tension from controversy, which can generate emotions and make the conversation more interesting. When a woman knows that you are only trying to say what you think she wants to hear, she will lose respect and trust in you. When you speak your mind freely to a woman, she will be attracted by your honesty. She will feel that she can trust and use what you say to accurately discover who you are as a person.

Women know that guys of actual value do not need to try hard. Showering a girl with unsolicited and undeserved compliments, favors and gifts makes it look like you are overcompensating for something else. It shows that you feel that you must provide incentives for a woman to be interested in you. This comes from a deep-seeded belief that you are not good enough as you are. A high quality man does not need to buy a woman's attention or affection, as he knows that he himself is enough.

Reflect deep inside and ask yourself: "From where is this action derived?" Does it come from a place of true altruism and a desire to provide value? Or are you actually bartering for something in return, such as a positive emotional response? Are your words sincere, or are you just telling someone what you think will make them happy?

3. Do not Chase or Force Rapport

You must always be willing to walk away from an interaction or have a woman leave you at any time. This shows a woman that you have abundance, self-respect and personal boundaries. You should remain calm and patient, and not be overly eager to pursue some underlying agenda. Some women especially enjoy being chased because of the sense of validation that it gives them. You instead want women to chase you, not vice versa. Be the flame not the moth. You cannot force attraction.

The act of chasing can take on many forms. The most literal form being you physically following a woman around like a puppy dog, or lunging after her and trying to convince her to stay talking with you. Common lines I hear from men include: "Just stay for *one* more drink."; "What?! You are leaving? But it is still so early." and "The real party is right here, where are you going?"

Likewise, refrain from sending pointless text messages to a woman between in-person interactions or repeatedly try to convince a woman to meet with you. If a woman wanted to meet with you, then she would prioritize the meeting and make it happen. At this point, it is extremely unlikely that you are going to convince her through the emotionless medium of text messaging. This type of behavior only communicates to a woman your lack of options and neediness.

You should lead a woman, not chase her. Instead of following a woman around a venue, take charge and lead her where you want to go. Be decisive in all your actions, including things such as choosing a restaurant, movie or how you want to spend the day. Indecisiveness is a huge turn off to most women. Women are more willing to forgive a bad decision than they are you being indecisive.

Related to chasing is the act of forcing rapport in a conversation. Forcing rapport is when you forcibly try to engage a person, instead of letting a conversation takes its natural course. Of course it may be in your best interest not to let the conversation die, but it should be prolonged in a more natural and non-forceful way. When one is forcing rapport, they are not speaking freely, but instead seeking a response after every statement they say. Conversely, you can generate attraction by leading a conversation and being unafraid to break rapport and steer the conversation in the direction of your choice.

Forcing rapport can occur when you are afraid of running out of things to say when speaking with a woman. Since a woman is giving you attention, you may feel that in return it is your duty to carry the conversation. This is the wrong mind frame to have. You should feel the same as when you are talking with your friends, and not be worried that only certain things are good enough to say. When unable to come up with something original to say, many men start immediately repeating back to a woman what she has just told them in order to fill the silence. This act of parroting a woman sounds something like this:

MAN: Hello, what's your name?

WOMAN: Kelly.

MAN: Kelly?

WOMAN: Yes.

MAN: Where are you from?

WOMAN: Montreal.

MAN: Oh, you're from Montreal. What are you doing here?

WOMAN: I'm here for a training meeting for work.

MAN: A work training meeting, you say ...

This type of parroting behavior should be avoided, since it is a manner of forcing rapport and shows that you are overly invested in keeping the conversation going. Instead, talk about whatever interests you. By doing this, you will be more likely to naturally infuse emotion into the conversation. When you are talking passionately about something, then those emotions will transfer onto the woman.

The ability to provide an honest and unfiltered conversation is much more important than the actual subject matter of the conversation. You will never run out of things to say if you are indifferent to the response that you will receive for saying them. This indifference tells a woman that you are not trying to impress her or seek her approval.

4. Do not Qualify Yourself / Try to Impress / Seek Reactions or Approval

A rich man does not have to tell you that he is rich. Bragging about anything makes you look insecure. Do not brag about your accomplishments, paycheck, car, the past women you have dated or how intelligent you are. Instead of appearing as someone of value, you come off as an insecure person who is actively touting his achievements in what is likely a preemptive attempt to overcompensate for unseen faults.

When you are actively trying to impress someone, you are communicating to them that your sense of self-worth comes from an external source. You feel that others must be made aware of your status, wealth or intellect, so that they will treat you with the respect and distinction which you feel that you deserve. It means that for you to feel confident, you must have your past accomplishments acknowledged. There is a difference between bragging and discussing with passion the things that you are proud of. The latter is preferable. If you really want to tell of an accomplishment, do so by either bring up the accomplishment indirectly in the course of telling a story or having someone else mention it about you.

Otherwise, you will come off as being reaction seeking. Reaction seeking is when you do or say something not from a place of honesty, but because you desire a particular response or reaction from another person. Normally, the sought after reaction is a sign of approval. An example being when a man uses self-deprecating humor to make others laugh at his own expense. Clearly such a joke is said not for one's own enjoyment, but to solicit a reaction from others. We have previously already touched on reaction seeking in regards to when one barters for attention. In this case, you are seeking a positive response for the drink, compliment, or favor you provided. Reaction seeking can even be present in the tone of your voice or the pause after a statement in which you are hoping to hear some form of approval.

Women can tell when you are reaction seeking and actively trying to solicit admiration from them. This behavior communicates to women that you are insecure and need their attention and approval. It tells a woman that you find it more important that she approves of you than you do trying to have an honest conversation. By seeking a woman's approval, you give her permission to define you and your worth. Do not be willing to sacrifice your own personal integrity for what others think of you. Do not try to impress, but express. Express yourself honestly and give others the opportunity to get to know the real you.

Trying to impress someone and being reaction seeking are symptoms of the broader need that you feel that you must qualify yourself to others. This need shows up in both you trying to qualify yourself in general, as well as qualify your individual beliefs, desires, actions and words. Below are some examples of the unattractive trait of qualifying oneself.

- If you feel that you must explain and defend every decision that you make to others.
- If your first response to a woman disagreeing with you is to immediately retract your statement because you are afraid of upsetting her.
- If a woman tells you that she hates your favorite musician, and you feel that you must justify your personal taste to her.

- If a woman dismisses an advance from you, and you respond by profusely apologizing, instead of respecting her decision while simultaneously remaining unashamed of your desire.

Directly qualifying yourself to a woman only further puts you into the frame of you being the seller and she the buyer. This frame should be avoided as much as possible. In situations where a woman finds you attractive, she may begin qualifying herself to you. If you hear the women start name/accomplishment dropping, this is a good sign. This means that she views you as having value and wants you to view her as being your equal. Women experience the act of qualifying themselves as a form of investment. Through qualification, they feel that they have worked to earn your approval. It is very important to leave room in a conversation for a woman to invest in one form or another. Women want to feel like that they have won you over, and that getting to be with you is their reward. People always appreciate more that which they have earned.

In addition to not actively seeking approval and positive reactions from others, you should also remain unreactive to any provocations that others throw at you.

5. Be Outcome Independent and Non-Reactive

Out of all the behaviors listed here, becoming non-reactive will likely take the largest amount of practice to achieve. Caring greatly about an outcome or having a disproportionate amount of investment early on in an interaction is advertised through the invested person being reactive. In an initial conversation where you barely know a woman, there is no good reason why the outcome should have a strong emotional effect on you. The opinion of a stranger does not shake the core confidence of an attractive man.

As previously mentioned in the chapter regarding scarcity, having mental and physical abundance greatly contributes to one being outcome independent. While the other bad behaviors on this list can more or less be immediately curtailed through conscious awareness, it's almost impossible to completely camouflage one's outcome dependence. Even if you are able to avoid reacting to a large degree, a small waver in eye contact, crack in vocal tonality or an interruption in the flow of your speech can give you away. For many women, even such a small show of incongruence will end any attraction.

Being able to hold one's composure while exposed to varied external stimuli demonstrates great self-confidence. As mentioned in the previous chapter, congruence tests are used to assess a person through checking their reactivity to different stimuli. A common congruence test is when a woman abruptly ends a conversation with you, runs over to start chatting with another man, and looks to see if you are needy enough to chase her. Even if you don't make the egregious error of physically lunging after her, an instantaneous look in your eyes that shows a fear of loss may still expose your outcome dependence.

When you are outcome dependent and acting reactively, it is normally shown via the four previously mentioned unattractive behaviors: breaking eye contact, bartering, chasing/forcing rapport and qualifying yourself. If a woman causes you to lose your train of thought or get stuck in your head via a congruence test, then you are being reactive. If you try to convince a woman who wants to go home to stay with you by shouting: "What you're leaving!? It's still early, how about one more drink?" then you are being reactive. If you continuously qualify yourself because you are worried of a woman's perception of you and that you may fall from her good graces, then you are being reactive.

Another common reactive trait is becoming "butt-hurt" when a woman does not positively reciprocate an advance. Being "butt-hurt" is a phrase that has only recently entered the American English vernacular and can be defined as when a person irrationally has their feelings hurt or shows unwarranted negative emotions over something that is trivial. An example would be if a person is unreasonably upset and hostile over their club football team being fairly defeated during a scrimmage game.

A common response when you have your feelings hurt or are rejected by someone is to strike back at them out of anger and resentment. They hurt you in some way, and you want to get even. However, a self-assured man living in abundance would feel no reason to do so. If you become visibly upset, angry or disappointed when a woman does not reciprocate interest in you, then you are being reactive and letting another person dictate your emotions. To a woman, this is incredible unattractive and demonstrates neediness and a lack of self-confidence.

Most importantly, being outcome independent allows a woman to feel comfortable around you. If a woman senses that you will not be upset or disappointed if she decides to leave you, then she will be more comfortable staying with you. On one level, the woman does not want to feel that she is responsible for your emotional state. She may not want to hurt your feelings or create awkwardness by rejecting your advances. On another lever, the woman is caring for her own personal safety.

A woman wants to know that if she chooses to spend time with you alone, but later decides against having a physical relationship, that you will be fully comfortable with her decision. Showing outcome independence towards a physical relationship is the best indicator that this truly will be the case. When a man is overly eager to buy a woman drinks or have her go with him somewhere, it advertises that he may have an underlying agenda which he is hoping to fulfill. A woman may then fear that this man will not respect her decisions regarding how their relationship is to evolve. In addition to being outcome dependent, being overly eager tells a woman that the man is likely inexperienced. A man who tries to force things along is usually trying to quickly close a deal before the other side figures out what is wrong with it.

To preemptively safeguard against ever potentially upsetting a woman, some men start seeking permission for every action they make. There are fewer behaviors which kill attraction faster than a man becoming a permission seeker. A man being terrified of upsetting a woman in anyway, or overly apologetic for the times in which he does, demonstrates incredible neediness. A woman wants a confident man who does not have to ask permission before he kisses her.

Many inexperienced men believe that if they show interest, e.g. trying to kiss a girl, and the girl does not reciprocate, then it is game over. The truth is that it all depends on your reaction to her reaction. If you go for a kiss and she turns her cheek to you, and you react by being hurt or overly apologetic, then it may likely be game over. If you react instead by smiling, and continue the conversation as if nothing had happened, then your self-confidence may generate more attraction than if you had actually kissed the woman in the first place.

By being unreactive, a woman will realize that you are a man who is showing honest intent, acting unapologetically, and is secure enough with himself that his emotions are independent from her own. Women do not want the added burden of being responsible for a man's emotions. Most women would prefer to tether themselves to a man who is well grounded and unreactive to the world around them. Women find attractive a man for whom the world reacts to him. Massive attraction is generated when you are unreactive to your environment or the congruence tests that a woman gives at you.

Do not constantly look to a woman for approval after every word you say. Do not immediately apologize or qualify yourself when a woman does not agree with you. Do not react to situations out of jealousy, to protect your ego or to validate yourself. The best reaction is often a lack of reaction. Being so well grounded and secure with oneself that the opinions of others don't faze you is incredibly attractive.

You should strive to be a man who is responsive, not reactive. A reaction is an involuntary retort to a stimulus, while a response is a coordinated and thought-out maneuver. While you cannot always control what happens to you, you can control your response. You are only reactive when you want something from another person, albeit even if it is only validation or positive emotions. If you were truly indifferent, then you would not be reactive or value seeking. If you come from a place where you are altruistically providing value to others, then you will never be reactive.

6. Provide Value (Do not Enter Interview Mode)

When you give without looking to get something in return, people will be more open to letting you into their lives. Bringing fun and positive energy to others will automatically make them more accepting of you. Provide value to entire groups of people, not just the women that you are interested in. The best frame to have is one which shows that you can offer value (fun, interesting conversation, nonjudgmental ear, useful advice, etc.) to a person or group and desire nothing in return for it. People naturally exclude those who they feel are trying to weasel their way into their party and leach value from them.

During your initial conversations with a woman, the value you offer can be as simple as just being a fun, honest, nonjudgmental and interesting person with whom she can talk. Try not to fill an initial conversation with questions that a company representative would ask you at a career fair. This is the typical default mode most guys enter when starting a conversation with a stranger.

This interview mode way of conversing usually sounds something like this:

MAN: Hello, I'm Tim. What is your name?
WOMAN: Elizabeth.
MAN: Are you a student?
WOMAN: Yes.
MAN: What do you study?
WOMAN: Chemistry.
MAN: Oh cool my cousin studies that, you must be very smart. Where are you from?
WOMAN: Montreal.
MAN: Montreal is such a cool city! I wish I lived there.

…

Dead on asking these types of interview questions without injecting any type of emotion or relevance is actually a subtle way of taking value from a woman. Instead of providing the woman with fun or intrigue, you are instead asking for her attention and then trying to further leach approval from her as you commend her on her answers to your questions. You are more interested in keeping the conversation going then you are to what she says. This is a form of forcing rapport.

Upon meeting a strange man, a woman's mind will immediately have the following three questions:

1. Who is this?
2. What does he want?
3. When will he leave?

If the answers that she comes up with are: some random creepy guy who has been hovering around me for the last thirty minutes, who desires my approval and attention while providing nothing in return, and does not look like he will be leaving soon; then the interaction may be dead on arrival. However, if she comes up with the answers: a super social guy who I have seen talking with everyone, who just wants to include me in his fun, and is not trying to trap me into a conversation; then the interaction will be off to a good start. It is completely unreasonable to expect a woman to entertain a complete stranger when she only senses that he wants something from her; such as her time, attention, approval or sex.

Not immediately entering interview mode will differentiate you from almost everyone else in a good way. Let this formal information naturally arise out of a more fun and interesting conversation. Experiment with not even exchanging names until after a girl first asks you for yours. At that point you can be sure that she will actually care what your name is. When you make statements instead of asking questions, you are providing more value. Making a statement shows insight into you as a person, and can provide value by being interesting, funny or triggering emotions. You come off more like a person who is just speaking their mind, and less like someone who is trying to force a rapport.

Likewise, try making assumptions about a woman instead of asking her direct questions. If your assumptions are correct, she will be impressed. If they are wrong, she will feel the need to correct them and qualify herself to you. For example, instead of replying with a simple yes or no answer, she may continue the conversation by asking why you think that she is from Montreal, etc. This qualification is an investment from her into the conversation and mirrors the type of qualifications women make when they are chasing a man. The more invested the woman gets in the conversation, and the greater desire she has for you to understand her, the farther down the road to attraction she goes.

7. Act Honestly / Show Congruence and Consistency

A woman finds nothing more infuriating and repulsive then discovering that a man is not who he appears to be. Many women's worst fear is being deceived. Women will date men that are known assholes because they know that these men's actions are true to their nature. A true asshole is actually much more appealing to women than a man who pretends to be an asshole or an asshole who pretends to be nice. Women want to be sure that they know what they are getting. Lying will often cause a woman to have a gut feeling that something is off about you, even if you are not actually caught in the lie. This feeling of uncertainty and being deceived will be a huge turn off to her.

You are not required to answer every question a women poses to you. You should have boundaries and not feel the need to jump through every hoop a woman puts in front of you. This does not mean to defensively deflect questions or hide behind jokes, but to show a willingness to break rapport and command the conversation. Leaving a sense of mystery about oneself, allows women to fill in your blanks using their own imagination shaped by their personal desires.

Lying is a way of hiding your true self behind a fake self. The only reason that you would lie is because you are ashamed that you are not good enough as you are, and feel the need to alter someone's perception of you in an attempt to gain their acceptance. The insecurity you show which makes you do this is probably way more unattractive than the facet of your life that you are trying to cover up.

Often we lie not with words, but indirectly through our behaviors and actions. Any incongruence between your thoughts, words and actions shows dishonesty. If you approach a woman under the false pretense of wanting to know the time, then you are lying to her. While your actual intent is that you want to meet her, you are simultaneously verbally throwing up a shield to protect your ego. This way you can save face if she does not immediately show interest back. However, unless you are very handsome or have social proof, why would you expect a woman to immediately find you attractive? By choosing to start a conversation with an incongruent lie, you are not demonstrating the attractive behaviors of a confident man, which would then allow attraction to grow.

We lie to hide the things about ourselves we perceive as being inadequate and to protect our self-image. Choosing to have personal integrity and fully accepting yourself as you are, opens the door to allow others to accept you. Women don't want a man who is perfect, but a man who is perfectly fine with himself. Acting with honest intent is one of the primary keys to attracting woman.

8. Interact as Man to Woman

There is a difference between making someone like you and generating attraction. The majority of men focus more on ensuring that a woman approves of them, rather than risking becoming vulnerable by honestly expressing themselves. Unapologetic honest expression of one's true self is at the core of what generates attraction. Thus by playing not to lose and to protect your ego, you are inevitably destined to lose. You need to be unapologetic about who you are as a person. It is OK and normal that not everyone will like you. When first approaching a woman, your intentions should be clear from the start. These intentions should simply be: "I want to get to know you."

Many men are ashamed and apologetic about the natural and normal attraction they have for women, and thus are not secure with their masculinity. Being sheepish or apologetic about your actions communicates to a woman that you feel that you are not good enough for her and that you are seeking her approval. However, being apologetic should not be confused with being empathetic. You should always be aware of other people's emotions and how you are making them feel. By being unapologetic, I mean that you should have personal integrity, be self-secure and not afraid of upsetting someone as a result of being honest about your beliefs and desires. This does not mean that you should lack empathy and be oblivious and callous to how others feel. Nor does it mean that you should not apologize upon making an honest mistake.

Showing empathy is actually an extremely powerful tool for building comfort with a woman. Showing empathy conveys to a woman that you are not a sociopath and that you are attuned to how she feels. When you see that you are making a woman uncomfortable, it is fine to apologize for the action that led to the discomfort. I actually recommend it. This shows to the woman that you are both attentive and respectful to her. This empathetic apology is different than being apologetic because you are ashamed of who you are as a person, or being apologetic over an honest statement from which a woman drew offence.

As a general rule, a woman's opinion of you will be heavily formed within your initial interactions together. After this point, it may take a lot of backtracking to be able to establish a more intimate relationship if she has already classified you as being unworthy of one. Try first asking a woman out on a date, and then getting to know her. This will establish the correct relationship frame right from the start, before you really get to know her and potentially develop deeper feelings. If you are deeply emotionally invested, before you even begin generating attraction with a woman, it will become harder to remain outcome independent.

Failure to confidently show interest, intent or escalate to a physical relationship with a woman will likely get you cast into the so called "friend zone." As soon as a woman shows some interest in you, show an appropriate amount of interest back. However, do so while not breaking any of the previous rules! It is also important to show a woman that she has earned your interest by something she has said or done, not simply because of her looks. Women want to know why you like them, and most do not want it only to be because of their physical appearance. Find something about the woman that you honestly admire and compliment her on that. This way your complement will be genuine. If you cannot find anything admirable about a woman — even after spending an extended amount of time with her — then she probably isn't the one for you.

In addition to the eight rules listed above, an additional important element of attraction is "relatability." Even if a woman feels massive amounts of attraction towards you, she may dismiss it if she does not find you relatable. When it comes to attracting women, the issue of relatability often appears at both ends of the learning curve. In the beginning, not being relatable will result in the failure to establish rapport or an emotional connection. In the end, after developing all the attractive traits and behaviors described thus far, you may have lost your relatability in the process.

You may have ended up crossing the entire identity spectrum and arrived on the other extreme. A woman may now view you as being so amazing that it is outside of *her reality* that you could ever desire or appreciate her. If a woman feels that you cannot relate to her, she may feel that you could never truly understand her. She may keep her guard up and prevent an emotional connection from forming. She may feel that the intimate act of opening herself up to you may be met by a wall of indifference.

You must show a woman that you understand and can relate to her on a personal level. The best way of becoming relatable is by being comfortable with showing your own vulnerabilities. Being vulnerable does not mean being weak or soft, but rather that you are strong enough to deal with the repercussions that may result from exposing your true self. There is no need for trying to always appear perfect. Women do not want to be with a man who is perfect. A woman does not want to feel that she can never relax or show any imperfections around you. Women don't care that you have flaws, only that you accept and don't try to hide them. Attractive women in particular are faced with a constant pressure to always appear perfect. Showing a woman that you will not judge her for being her true self around you is one of the greatest gifts that you can give her.

Chapter 9: Conservation of Energy and Momentum

"The law of conservation of energy tells us that we can't get something for nothing, but we refuse to believe it."
-Isaac Asimov

Now that you have been taught the core principles behind attraction, you need to take the steps necessary to fully internalize them. It is not enough to just know something. Your actions must be derived from firmly fortified internal beliefs. If this book has done its job, then it has rationalized concepts that on the surface may seem irrational or counterintuitive. However, until you start operating in the world by the principles detailed thus far, your brain will not fully believe them. The mind requires you to complete the feedback loop so that the principles can be fully internalized.

This means that you must leave your comfort zone and start interacting with many new women. You will not see immediate results just from reading this book. However, you will be able to accurately reflect on your interactions and understand the social dynamics which are taking place. Remember, failing does not equate to failure. Every new experience will give you the chance to learn and identify your personal sticking points and strengths. The thing required most for learning any new skill is self-discipline.

In theory, the greater action you take, the sooner you will start seeing results. This is predominately true, with the following two caveats. Simply going through the motions — without applying knowledge and critically reflecting on the outcome — will not lead to better results. You can instead inadvertently reinforce bad habits this way. Secondly, it is more important to aim for sustainable progress than sporadic achievement. The diet that works the best is the one that is both practical and sustainable. Fasting might provide you with good results for a week, but it is definitely not sustainable in the long term. Likewise, your routine for bettering your social skills over the long term also needs to be both practical and sustainable.

When I started, I personally treated every Friday and Saturday night as I would a required university class. No matter how I felt, I forced myself to commute 90 minutes to a bar in a larger city to spend four hours socializing before commuting 90 minutes back home. Given my work obligations, geographic location and public transportation times, this was the best that I could manage. However, after a year I had dug myself out of scarcity, had very consistent results and was dating multiple women a week.

If you can afford the time, I would recommend scheduling in more social activities per week. Even dinners out with friends can be useful to break trends of social isolation and boost your social mood. Like any other skill, social skills need to be worked out. While bars and clubs are useful because of the high concentration of available women, they are by no means the only places where you can go. Online websites which organize events, such as Meetup or Couchsurfing, provide great alternatives. I would recommend not drinking alcohol during the nights out which you treat as "training nights," since it may impede your routine's sustainability both financially and health-wise. Plus, you do not want to become reliant on alcohol as a crutch when you want to socialize.

When starting out, the only metric I gave myself for success was that actually I went out and to the best of my ability stayed in conversation with women the entire time. I was only hard on myself the nights where I would chicken out and not approach anyone. These squandered nights also made the additional three hours of commute time a waste. The secret to becoming successful with women is no different than the secret to finding success in anything. At the end of the day, it all boils down to persistently taking action. In the words of basketball star Michael Jordan:

"I can accept failing, but I can't accept not trying."

It is important to choose the right metrics for measuring progress and success. Evaluate yourself by asking the following questions: "Did I push myself out of my comfort zone?"; "Was I speaking and acting honestly?"; "How did I make the other person feel?"; "How did I feel?"; "Which unattractive behaviors was I displaying, and what caused them?"

Even small steps add up over long enough time periods. Real change will appear over the course of weeks and months, not necessarily days. Within a year, you may not be able to even conceive how you had issues with women in the first place. A key to making a plan sustainable is learning to enjoy the process. If you are loathing going out and interacting with new people, it will be difficult to keep the habit going. You will come off as not being genuine if you are treating each conversation as a means to an end. Additionally, any negative emotions that you emit will poison your interactions.

Being able to sustain a positive energy and attitude is imperative for maximizing consistency and success. This can be incredible hard to do if you are still reliant on drawing your emotional state from external sources. You cannot let any negative emotions from one interaction fester and infect future interactions. You should never take personally the emotional states of others, since they are determined by an infinite number of external factors.

Women feed off the energy in their environment, and will actively surround themselves with the people that they find to be the most positive and fun. By absorbing the positive energy radiating from others, a woman's own emotional state will rise. Dancing and singing with friends are common methods women use to pump their own emotional states.

In social gatherings, the real currency for attracting women is not money but fun. In terms of value, buying a girl a drink comes nowhere close to providing her with a fun and exciting evening. Would you turn away someone who offered to bring excitement and fun into your life? The vast majority of women who you cold-approach (approach without prior introduction) will initially feel no attraction towards you. Until attraction begins to build, your initial offer can be an opportunity to share in the fun that you are currently having.

While being in a positive state is ideal, you should never force it. It is more important to be congruent by fully accepting the current mood that you are in. The rare offering of an honest conversation is often in itself enough for a woman to appreciate your company. However, through knowing oneself, you can proactively take the actions necessary to transition yourself into a more positive emotional state. Since state is transferable, it is good to put yourself in the same state that you want the woman you approach to be in. This state being: social, fun and relaxed.

When a woman enters a venue, she will subconsciously note to herself the people who appear interesting. If you are standing in the corner, not smiling and clenching your beer to your chest, she may not even register your existence. Even worse, she may register you as looking pathetic, and hold it as a preconceived notion against you when you initially approach her. This is an example of negative social proof.

Now imagine that the same woman enters the venue and sees you surrounded by other people with whom you are smiling, joking and laughing in the throes of an entertaining conversation. In this scenario, she will register in her mind that you look like a fun guy. Now when you initially approach her, she will be more inclined to find out what you are all about. A man could be "rejected" by a woman early on in a night only to have the woman throw herself at him later due to his then increased positive emotional state.

While you should try to provide positive energy, you should never become a "dancing monkey" whose actions are motivated solely for a woman's entertainment; i.e. you should never be bartering for a woman's attention. You should always be acting through your own honest intentions and focusing on your own enjoyment. Positive energy should flow out of you in all directions and draw others to you.

We are all familiar with how it feels to be in a low energy state. It is the feeling we have after finishing a long day at the office, or pulling an all-nighter before an exam. When in this state, it is natural to want to just sit back, relax and forget about the world. However, we also know those golden moments in life when everything seems to perfectly align. We feel in the zone and confident that we can take on whatever next might be thrown at us. We enter a mental state of flow in which success seems almost effortless. I am sure you have felt it at least once during a sport's game, in a work meeting, or while acing an exam. While we may not be able to tap into that energy whenever we desire, with proper practice we can learn to more rapidly and consistency enter this state.

After spending 8 to 10 hours staring a computer screen or textbook in isolation, especially while working on complex tasks which require laser focus, the human mind is about as far removed as possible from being in a fun and social state. Unfortunately for many of us, this has become our default state. After a week filled with back to back days like these, even going out on a Friday night may seem like more work than fun. Especially if we plan to use that time to overcome anxiety and push our comfort zone to meet women. Many people choose to use alcohol as a way to unwind and more easily transition to a more social state. A more sustainable and comprehensive solution than alcohol is to work out our social skills and build momentum.

The more often we transition from a lower to higher energy state, the easier it becomes. Our neural pathways for being social will grow wider as the process becomes more routine. When entering a venue, I recommend starting a conversation with a stranger as soon as possible, preferably a pretty woman. Talking with your friends will not give you the same adrenaline kick and challenge as when trying to engage a pretty stranger. Even if the conversation fizzles out, which will often happen early on in a night, you will have still boosted your energy and started building momentum. By the time you enter your third or fourth conversation of the night, you will likely find yourself in a much higher state of flow. This micro-momentum that you build every time that you go out can scale to macro-momentum in longer periods of your life.

By having initiative and repeatedly taking action, you can lengthen the periods of time in which you feel in the zone, while shorting the time it takes to transition into this state. Fueled by a wave of confidence from rapid improvement, you will likely have periods of extended success. But even these great peaks will eventually subside, and you must remember that it takes conscious effort to sustain momentum. The easiest way to keep up momentum and consistent growth is to build a life that naturally supports it.

Chapter 10: Master Theory of Attraction

"Confidently, unapologetically and assertively show your honest intent to a woman while simultaneously remaining outcome independent."

The above theory clearly defines in one statement why some men are successful with women while others fail. While it may seem simple on the surface, on a deeper level this statement encompasses all the previous principles mentioned thus far. Without a thorough understanding of the previous chapters, this theory can easily be wrongly interpreted and erroneously applied. The theory can be broken down into its two parts: showing honest intent and being outcome independent.

Honesty has been a staple principle throughout this entire book. When being truly honest, your conduct is fully congruent and consistent; ergo your thoughts, words and actions are continuously aligned. Showing honest intent is synonymous with acting in a man to woman frame. Men who try to hide their interest or are ashamed of their desires are acting dishonestly. By acting like a friend, these men only ever become a woman's friend. Every time you spend time with a woman that you like and hide your interest, you are actively lying to her. Dishonesty tells a woman that you are either faking who you are in order to hide your inadequacies or are trying to manipulate her into liking you. These behaviors stem from an internal belief that you are not good enough as you are.

Being honest extends well past your interactions with woman and into how you choose to live your life. While it is important to be honest with others, it is also critical that you are honest with yourself. Perhaps by now you have realized that the same core beliefs it takes to be successful with women mirror those needed to be successful in life. All the attractive traits and behaviors mentioned in this book are beneficial to you regardless of your interest in attracting women. Your attractiveness to women comes as a consequence of improving yourself as a man. You become an attractive man by living a life of authenticity and integrity.

You become authentic when you are pursuing your purpose, and living your life in accordance to what you value. Even if you lack what others would define as "success," you keep your integrity by knowing that you are acting true to yourself. This is the deepest form of honesty. You accept yourself as you are. You do not lie to yourself to protect your ego. You work at becoming who you want to be, not what others have determined as being worthy of praise, love or approval. Fulfillment, confidence and self-respect come from living a life that is in line with your values. When you show how much you value and respect yourself, you gain the admiration of others. Lead a life that you are proud of, and thus a woman who shares your values would be proud to join.

Being outcome independent means that no matter the response a woman has to your advances, the outcome does not affect how you feel about yourself. By remaining completely secure through temporary "rejections," you show the highly attractive traits of confidence and lack of neediness. As one pulls themself out of scarcity and into abundance, one naturally becomes more outcome independent.

Outcome independence stems from believing that you are enough as you are. This is the deepest form of abundance. If you are truly content with yourself, then you do not require validation, approval or positive reactions from others. When others sense this, they know that you are not seeking any type of value from them, and that having you in their lives can thus be beneficial. This also puts them at ease by indicating that you will not burden them with being responsible for your emotional state.

Showing honest intent means that you are willing to express to a woman your interest in her. Outcome independence means that you are completely comfortable accepting that a woman may be unreceptive. Persistence often works with an available woman when you act with honest intent and are outcome independent. Women admire persistence when it illustrates the healthy sense of entitlement of a man who is confident of what he wants, but who also does not become emotionally distraught upon not getting it. This fulfills a woman's wish to feel desired, but not in a needy value seeking sort of way. Any type of persistence which lacks honest intent and outcome independence will instill disinterest, discomfort and even fear in women.

Your journey of self-improvement should be motivated by a desire to be the best that you can be, rather than from a place where you feel the need to prove something to someone else. If you are searching for fulfillment, you will need to find it inside yourself. You will never find lasting fulfillment in a woman or society at large. Trying to acquire it from external sources will only lead you on an endless pursuit. True fulfillment comes from embracing the never ending process of pursuing your self-avowed personal goals.

For long term success, you will need to build a life in accordance to your values which supports and reinforces the lifestyle that you want. Unnecessary struggle can be avoided by having your beliefs, desires and actions all aligned. The women in your life will be a reflection of your life. By taking personal responsibility and working towards becoming the man you want to be, you become the man that women want to be with.

Read more at:

www.trueanomaly.org

Made in the USA
Middletown, DE
29 August 2017